Acknowledgements

For a person trained in electrical engineering, writing a narrative is as foreign of a thought as selling pretzels in China. Both are not easy, I assure you. Only through the immense support and encouragement of numerous people did this project come to fruition. Many thanks go out to Faiz Ahmad, who selflessly offered his time and editorial skills in reading the early drafts of messy notes and rambling stories. Few are lucky enough to have friends like him. Laura Grant and JoSelle Vanderhooft did wonders to shape the direction of the book. I am grateful to my agent Carol Mann and her team (Eliza Derier and Myrsini Stephanides) for showing enthusiasm and taking on this project with me. So many others have offered great suggestions that have been incorporated that I will invariably miss some names, though here is a very short list: Tina Chou, Joshua Martino, Charles Hsieh, Stacey Choe, Lily Shu, Kirby Carder, and Noch Noch Li.

Joseph Sze has been an incredible business partner not only in his abilities and dedication, but in his constant support. The experiences in this book are as much his as they are mine. I am lucky to consider Joe and his wife my second family.

To my parents, siblings, and all the in-laws, I cannot thank you enough for the constant support and advice through these years in China.

Karen, my beautiful wife, was there through it all. She was always the unbiased sounding board and remained strong for the entire family. To Kayla and my yet-to-be-born son, this story will tell you why daddy brought the family to China.

The China Twist

by wen-szu lin

Cover designs by Laura Grant

ISBN-10: 0615703518

ISBN-13: 978-0615703510

BC Publishing

Author's Note

This is a work of nonfiction. All materials, depictions, recollections, and opinions represented in this book are solely that of the author. Certain names, characteristics, and details have been changed to protect the identities of those involved.

Table of Contents

Introduction

Nineteen thousand kilograms. Forty-two thousand pounds. Five thousand bags. Twenty-five thousand pretzels. This is how much Auntie Anne's Pretzel Mix would fit inside one forty-foot shipping container. And we might have to dump it all down the drain. Literally. One bag at a time.

Our assigned Chinese customs agent, Mr. Zeng, proposed the complete destruction of the entire container if the next sample of our pretzel mix did not pass his department's inspections. Full destruction entailed opening up one bag of flour at a time, slowly pouring the contents into the drain, and hosing down the flour with water to ensure the drain did not clog. Finding a special drain large enough to wash down the water and flour mix would not be easy. We knew. We had to dump over six hundred kilograms of caramel already.

The customs inspection report stated that our first failed sample of the pretzel mix contained bacteria found only in dairy products. Given that the pretzel mix contained only flour, salt, and sugar, finding dairy bacteria in this product amounted to a modern day miracle. But I had to say bravo to Mr. Zeng and his team of advanced food scientists. They had become so proficient in finding chemicals like melamine in milk powder that they could now detect whatever they wanted in samples. Our attempts to explain the impossibility of the scenario ended in failure. Mr. Zeng threatened to fail the shipment outright if we continued to challenge his authority. We had just opened the first Auntie Anne's Pretzels store in China and we were about to get shut down.

✿ ✿ ✿

In mid-2007, my business partner Joseph Sze and I received a life-changing email: an official notice that granted us the Chinese master franchise rights for Auntie Anne's Pretzels. Re-reading each word more than three times, I celebrated alone, dreaming of the immense changes to my life that were to come—moving around the world to China, embracing my destiny of being an entrepreneur, savoring every experience, good or bad. I relived that moment with fond memories, though my path could not have been more different than what I had dreamed.

An investor once warned us that "opening a business in China is like experiencing Chinese water torture." A "China Twist," so to speak. A fitting description, given that we were opening a pretzel chain.

The concept behind Chinese water torture was simple. Immobilize a victim. Drip water on the victim. Repeat. Again. And again. And again.

The preferable place is the forehead; the victim could see it coming. Make sure the drips came at irregular times. Cold water shocks; it creates imbalance from a person's natural temperature. The only certainty is that there would be a next drip; the anticipation would haunt the victim exponentially.

Drip. Repeat. Again. And again. And again. That is it. Watch the victim go insane.

Introduction

I cannot pinpoint when the drips started. Quitting my job definitely set them in motion, but, no, they did not start then. Moving to China without knowing the culture or the language felt like the first drop, but they did not start there, either. It is not true what they say about water torture though, that it takes a long time to take effect. The first bout of insanity started rearing its ugly head within months of being in China.

Drip. Incapacitating our entire staff during training. Drip. Employees threatening physical violence against other employees. Drip. Getting ordered by different government bureaus to make contradictory modifications to the stores. Drip. Getting constantly picked on by the Customs bureau. Drip. Employees abusing local labor laws to take advantage of us. Drip. Hiding from our employees in fear of our personal safety. Drip, drip, drip...

Drip 1

Pretzels in China?

What Does Melamine Have to Do With Us?

By December of 2008, Joe and I had been living in China for nearly a year, working hard to open the Auntie Anne's Pretzels franchise in Beijing. Joe and I had become friends at the University of Pennsylvania's Wharton School while obtaining our MBAs. Joe and I kept in touch as we entered the corporate world in management consulting and private equity. We talked a lot about entrepreneurship while we were in school, and we found an opportunity to work together through Auntie Anne's Pretzels.

Throughout 2007, we applied for and won the master franchise rights to Auntie Anne's for mainland China, and raised a small fund to pilot the concept. We moved to China in early 2008. Waving goodbye to my wife at the airport, where we had just returned from our honeymoon, I hauled my life in the form of two overstuffed suitcases to the freezing, gray winter of Beijing. Joe and his wife had arrived there two weeks earlier and had rented an inexpensive one-bedroom apartment for me downstairs from their new home. They bought their first meal in China from a 7-Eleven and ate it in their dark, cold living room; they had yet to figure out the pre-pay systems for purchasing electricity, hot water, and gas. Yet they adapted to China quickly, and gave me the condensed tutorial on basic Beijing living when I landed.

One of our first priorities was to import the pretzel mix from Gap, Pennsylvania, which was the home of Auntie Anne's headquarters. The recipe for Auntie Anne's Pretzels had been a trade secret for all twenty years of the brand's existence. Every Auntie Anne's pretzel in the world is made using the same recipe.

Our initial plan was simple: import several key ingredients, including the pretzel mix, powdered pretzel flavors, and a few sauces. We received our first shipment at the end of June, 2008. The goods left customs quickly, which I assumed was positive news. In China, clearing imports involves two steps. First, customs would inspect and collect customs taxes on the products. Customs only cared about collecting taxes. Second, a separate department, called CIQ (China Inspection and Quarantine Bureau), was responsible for clearing all food products for usage in China. They were an equivalent of a health bureau for imported items. Manyun, our importing firm responsible for the paperwork and approvals, recommended that we start using the food we had imported, despite the fact that CIQ had not cleared them. This was normal practice, they said, and they had never seen any products fail in their ten years of experience.

Manyun was wrong.

We provided samples for each product to CIQ, and from June to August, there was no news or updates. Then, I received an urgent email and call from Manyun. Believe it or not, this was one of the most coherent emails I received from them over the years.

Dear Mr Lin,

Sorry to bother you, but this is urgent.

4

The Caramel Dip we import get something problem. The CIQ found the sorbic acid contains this item is about 4.9% which the CIQ standard in China should below about 1.09%. So the CIQ need to seal up for keeping the Caramel Dip. If the result is still disqualified, the Caramel Dip should finally be send back to the country of exportation or apply to be destroyed.

Liz

Beijing Manyun international logistics co ltd

August 27, 2008

Liz's follow up phone call backtracked on their recommendations that we could start using the shipment, stating now that we must not use any part of the shipment until we received CIQ approval.

CIQ found that our caramel had a sorbic acid (a preservative) level that was nearly five times higher than the regulation limit. Auntie Anne's headquarters was able to show documentation that the same batch was tested by the manufacturer well within the acceptable range for this preservative before leaving port. Sorbic acid levels were inherent in the dip and could not change drastically with time or under different environmental conditions. Therefore, the reported increase was a physical impossibility.

CIQ instructed us to go immediately with one of their agents to quarantine our products. When I arrived at the CIQ office the following day, I was directed to a room of cubicles where our agent, Mr. Zeng, sat. The CIQ office was located in an industrial area, home to many storage warehouses in the south part of Beijing. An old building with paint peeling off the outside walls and cracked windows caked with dust, the CIQ office felt sad and did not resemble a government building. Privileged college graduates would not dream of working in such a run-down place, yet this was precisely where Mr. Zeng had been assigned for his first government job.

Mr. Zeng sat facing me, and appeared to be working intently on his computer. But he saw and acknowledged me when I waved at him. Unlike many of the older, unkempt government officials I saw on the way in, Mr. Zeng had a clean-cut look about him, with fair, smooth, pale skin that exhibited his youth and innocence. His face was on the long side, but not abnormally so, with hair that was tidy and combed to the right, despite looking like it had never met gel or hair spray. In terms of looks, the best word to describe him was normal, with no distinctive or memorable features. Not handsome, not ugly, not tall or short, not fat, but skinny like many other Chinese men; a typical face and build that would have blended in with any local Chinese crowd. He wore a typical light blue government-issued jacket and dark blue pants.

He looked busy, his expression serious as he stared at the screen in front of him, squinting to see what must have been small text. I was thoroughly impressed by his concentration, unexpected for a government employee. After waiting by the door for a few seconds, he shot a quick glance over at me.

"Please wait for a few minutes as I finish up my work," he said in a deep, professional voice.

"No problem," I tried to say cheerfully and nonchalant, wanting to make a good first impression. I relaxed a bit and took the opportunity to look around the office. The three other inspectors in the room were hard at work on their computers too. In addition to the four or five cubicles in the fifty-square-meter room, there were some bookshelves and one long conference table. The shelves and table were filled with packaged food items, from wine bottles to canned foods to candies. They must receive many samples, I thought.

Empty cookie and chocolate candy wrappers littered each inspector's desk, all from the same company called Crai, an Italian firm that wanted to launch a group of restaurants and grocery stores in China at that time. A good friend of mine who headed up Crai's importing had been complaining to me about the lengthy process at CIQ for months. Specifically, she mentioned several items that had been rejected and 'destroyed' by CIQ: cookies and chocolate candies. What a coincidence, I thought as I looked at the crumb-covered desks. I sure hope that these customs agents did not hurt their stomachs during the 'destruction' process.

After my quick visual tour of the room, Mr. Zeng was still not finished. He still had the same razor-sharp focus on his computer, but now I noticed that he was not typing with both hands, and instead had one hand navigating the mouse. The mouse crisscrossed the mouse pad in a frenzy. What was he using? Excel model? Proprietary customs software?

An explosion answered my question.

Faint sounds crackled and exploded from his computer. I leaned in and listened carefully. *Shhuuuu....boom! Boom. Boom. Crack, pop, pop, pop. Boom!!!* That was not music. It was the sounds of guns and bombs going off! I realized. Mr. Zeng continued wriggling the mouse, clicking on its buttons while his left hand tapped the space bar and several letter keys with lightning speed. I envied his focus. I could see his screen reflected in the window behind him. His computer monitor was full of monsters trying to kill each other. Warcraft! Well, a Chinese version of it. Mr. Zeng was not working tirelessly to clear as many customs forms as possible before the Olympics—he was playing computer games.

Sweat formed on his forehead after about five minutes into his marathon session. Fifteen minutes in, the sweat started rolling down the left side of his face.

Meanwhile, the reflections in the window gave me a full view of other inspectors' screens. One inspector preferred red blouses to green ones, and seemed like an adept shopper from the many windows she had opened to compare similar products across several websites. The next inspector had true, raw talent as well as commendable organization skills. He had ten small instant messenger windows placed evenly and symmetrically from the top left of his screen to bottom right. Conversations flowed smoothly and quickly across all ten. I could type nearly 100 words per minute, but I was no match for this inspector. I silently applauded his talent in keeping up with so many screens, and making it seem effortless.

After Mr. Zeng finished his "work," he got up and walked to a filing cabinet in the corner of the room.

"Give me five more minutes and I will be ready." He opened the file cabinet, pulled out a duffle bag, and headed to another room. A few minutes later, he returned wearing casual clothes: jeans and a dark polo shirt.

"Let's go," he said, duffle bag over his shoulder. Then he turned towards the online shopper. "Li Ming, I have a busy afternoon with inspections. I will head home afterwards. See you tomorrow." It was 2:00 p.m.

"So, how are you doing today?" I opened cautiously in the taxi after we settled in, wanting to feel out his personality and attitude before trying to engage him.

"Busy day. We have so many cases that we have to finish up before the Olympics. It has been non-stop. Very tiring," Mr. Zeng explained.

"Yeah, of course. Everyone wants to import into China, so I can see why you are so busy," I responded, with a sudden urge to ask him about his Warcraft game. Changing my mind, I quickly moved on to the next topic. "Are you from Beijing?"

"No, I am from the South. I actually went to school in England and studied there for a few years, in a small town a little bit outside of London," he announced with no small amount of pride. "I returned to China about two years ago."

"Oh, you studied in England! That is great." I switched from Mandarin to English, hoping that using English could be a point of connection.

He looked at me with a blank stare. He, obviously, had absolutely no clue what I had said. Oftentimes, I spoke a little fast, so I tried again, only much slower and enunciating each word clearly. "How did you like your time in England?"

Blank stare. An annoyed look crossed his face.

I had to switch tactics again. I returned to speaking Mandarin. "Did you enjoy your time in England?"

"Oh yeah," he jumped in enthusiastically. "It was a lot of fun. School work was pretty easy, so I got to enjoy touring the area and was able to hang with friends." I wondered if his classes had been taught in Chinese. "It is not like this job, constantly stressful and busy. I wish I were back in school again."

Probably trying not to be rude, he followed up with his own questions. "So where did you grow up? Your accent is not from the mainland."

These questions were usually tricky. Sound too foreign and people would take advantage. Sound too local and you might not get the leeway granted to foreigners. I decided in this case to play the dumb foreigner.

"I am from the US. I grew up in Washington, DC." I did not want to talk about myself, so I changed the topic again. "It sure is hard to do business in China," I said, wanting to draw sympathy. "Things like these customs issues and health bureau issues are all foreign to me."

Mr. Zeng listened closely while nodding his head slowly in agreement. He paused for a few seconds, apparently to think. "Yes, it sure is different here. Guanxi [relationships] and friends are important here, if you know what I mean. Many Westerners come in here thinking that the system can operate as it did in their countries. They are wrong.

To succeed, you must have friends. Friends and guanxi are developed through practices that have been around for thousands of years—like gift-giving and helping out each other. These practices will not change that quickly," he lectured, and looked into my eyes. "I can teach you."

Now we were getting somewhere! "Yes Sir, I think that you can be a great teacher!" I had no idea why I instantly switched over to calling this kid a "Sir." "It would be great to learn from you. You seem to be very experienced in government and business." I tried a bit of flattery for kicks. Man, I was on a roll, so why stop there? "Sir, compared to me, your expertise in the Chinese culture and business environment would be so valuable. I would love to learn a little bit of your expertise."

Sir Zeng looked like he was enjoying this line of conversation, but of course there had to be something in it for him. "How about this? My English is pretty good already, but it can always improve. It would be good to have someone to speak English on a regular basis with," he offered.

A conversation partner? With me? I would be speaking to myself, I thought.

"What are you doing this weekend?" he continued. "Why don't we have coffee and I can teach you about Chinese Customs Bureau practices, and you can help me practice my English?"

Hmm…would learning about Chinese customs involve learning about how to give bribes discreetly? "Sure, let's do that!" I offered with genuine enthusiasm. "Let's exchange numbers, and I will give you a call this weekend." Coincidentally, we were arriving at the warehouse as we exchanged numbers. I was amazed. Had I negotiated passing our caramel inspections for English lessons?

As we walked into the warehouse, I suddenly remembered that the latest notice from Manyun warned us not to use any part of our shipment. Our shipment included the pretzel mix that we had already started using. We had finished about half of one crate but had nine other untouched crates here. I was praying that the used pretzel mix crate was not next to the caramel dips. But it was.

As we walked alongside the crates, we stopped at the one that contained the caramel dip. Mr. Zeng looked at the ten large, white buckets of dip and took out a clipboard to start filling out paperwork. After finishing the forms a few minutes later, he took out a roll of yellow tape that reminded me of the barricade tapes on TV with the words "Quarantine!" on it and started to wrap it around the buckets. He looked like he was sectioning a crime scene off for forensics.

"Did you know that it is illegal for you to use any part of the shipment without my, well, the CIQ's approval?" Mr. Zeng warned, with a hard, stern look on his face and a deepened voice. "In fact, based on CIQ regulations, you can be fined many times the cost of the goods. It is a serious offense."

At this point, his gaze turned away from me to the half-empty crate of pretzel mix next to us.

Message received. Let us increase the number of English lessons, I thought. Mr. Zeng looked away and handed over a form for me to sign. "This form is to confirm that the caramel dip has been quarantined and you cannot use it." He ignored the pretzel mix and started to head out. "Let's go, it's late." Yeah, it was late: it was about 3:00 p.m.

"By the way, instead of taking me back to the office, can you drop me off at home?" Mr. Zeng demanded. His house was nowhere near the office, and it was a long, expensive taxi ride. On the way to his house, we chatted about random, lighthearted topics. Before he got out of the car, he said, "Remember, let's try to meet up to talk. We should become friends. Send another sample of caramel dip to our office, and we will take care of it."

Over the next few weeks, I texted and called Mr. Zeng, trying to meet up with him for coffee, for drinks, and even for dinner. He always found a polite way to decline the offer. In reality, I must have failed whatever test he was giving me.

I thought the whole caramel issue was over. But then, about a month later, I received a call from Mr. Zeng.

"Hello, Mr. Lin," Mr. Zeng began, with a much more formal voice than when we were chatting in the car. "Unfortunately, I must inform you that the second sample you gave me did not pass. The sorbic acid level still measured beyond our regulated limit. Based on Chinese regulations, you have two choices. You can either destroy the shipment or ship it back to the US."

Mr. Zeng's cold attitude surprised me as he explained the details of the tests. He spoke as if we had never met before. We had 600 kg—just over 1,300 lbs.—of caramel (well, 550 kg since we had used a portion of it already), and this guy wanted us to destroy it.

"Mr. Zeng, from what you said, your own testing results on the second sample varied by over 70 percent! If there is so much variation in your own tests, how can you trust this result?" I pleaded with him.

"I performed the tests myself," he said, with agitation in his voice. Then, he challenged with an impossible question: "Are you saying what I did was incorrect?!"

"Of course I would never imply anything like that," I replied, trying to hold back my anger at this ridiculous situation. I calmed down and said in a lower, stable voice. "Come on, my friend, I am only trying to say that there may be other reasons for these results—such as the testing equipment becoming accidentally contaminated by other samples."

"No! The situation is out of my hands now. I have submitted the paperwork to my superiors. Bottom line, it does not matter if my results had differed by 10,000 percent. What is important is that your samples failed twice. There is nothing further I can do. This caramel dip either needs to be destroyed under the supervision of our people, or it needs to be shipped out."

And with that, our caramel dip's fate was sealed. Bye-bye, Auntie Anne's Caramel Dip in China. You are not fit for Chinese consumers.

CIQ sent another agent out the following week who sat with our manager as he opened one bucket of caramel at a time and dumped it down the drain. The dip's gooey thickness made the process very difficult and time-consuming. They spent two hours dumping it all.

We thought then that we were done with the CIQ. Again, we were wrong.

A few months after the caramel incident, we received our second shipment. Our pretzel mix came in without issue on the first shipment, and our second shipment consisted of 100 percent pretzel mix. After paying the full custom tax and receiving the shipment in our warehouse, we received the following email:

Hello Mr. Lin,
We have communicate with MR ZENG this morning. He informed us that the pretzel mix (8lb and 4lb) contains something named pathogenic bacteria (致病菌). This is the reason causing the disqualification.
Liz
Beijing Manyun international logistics co ltd
December 5, 2008

Are you kidding me? This situation was spiraling out of control. If our second shipment got rejected, then this brand was pretty much done for. Auntie Anne's relied on this main ingredient (as pretzel mix was, undoubtedly, a key element to actually making pretzels), and it had to be imported directly from Pennsylvania. As the email mentioned, it seemed like that CIQ had discovered a dairy bacteria in our pretzel mix.

How were they able to detect dairy bacteria in a pretzel mix that had absolutely no dairy content? I was not sure what type of game this Mr. Zeng guy was playing, but we needed to resolve it.

As we dug into the issue, we learned that our logistics manager messed up when he prepared the sample from the second shipment. He delivered to the CIQ a sample from the first shipment of pretzel mix, which CIQ had already tested and found to be fully within Chinese regulations. Essentially, the pretzel mix that passed a few months earlier had now failed the inspection. Lovely.

Before we gave them a second sample, we needed to understand exactly what had happened. If the second sample failed, then there would be no more samples and no hope for recovering this shipment. My first attempts to befriend Mr. Zeng were not successful, so I did not want any more direct contact. So we started calling and talking to everyone we knew to see who had relationships with CIQ, and preferably someone higher ranked than Mr. Zeng. We contacted our entire investor list and informed them that if we could not pass this shipment, then we would have to close shop in China. We called friends and friends of friends who owned restaurants in Beijing. We asked our local registration agents for help in figuring out who knew people in the CIQ. We informed the US Commerce Department in Beijing of our situation and asked our contacts to have them call into CIQ for us. We used every last connection that we had to figure out how to reach the CIQ personnel.

In late 2008, China was rocked by the milk scandal, wherein most of the country's top milk and infant formula manufacturers were implicated in selling products laced with a chemical called melamine. Melamine is a type of plastic known for its flame retardant properties and used in such products as counter tops and dry erase boards. Nitrogen-rich, melamine can make food products appear high in protein if added. Tens of thousands of babies and kids in China fell sick after drinking this milk, and several died from exposure. Milk-related products were pulled throughout China. One large milk company, Sanlu, bankrupted. The government executed two perpetrators and jailed dozens.

We had the opportunity to have dinner with the US Ambassador's wife around this time. When I brought up our situation, she chuckled and responded apologetically, "Sorry boys, we are stopping a lot of their shipments in the US. They must be doing this to you to retaliate." That was no comfort to us, because we still faced the possibility that our stock of pretzel mix, enough to fill a forty-foot container, might get destroyed.

We struggled over what to do next for weeks and had many face-to-face meetings with advisors and agents to learn their take on the situation. No one had any good suggestions for us. Most people mentioned that they knew people in the CIQ, but those people turned out to be CIQ personnel who worked in other cities. We did have a few contacts who knew Mr. Zeng's boss, and they made some calls for us, but we did not hear any responses. "Good luck" was the most useful direct feedback that we received.

However, much to our surprise, one of our contacts must have made a convincing call on our behalf without telling us. About a month after the whole issue started, I received a call from Mr. Zeng. He was very cordial and extremely nice on the phone.

"Congratulations!" he exclaimed, "Your second sample passed! Please feel free to use your imported items at any time now." With that, our problems with the CIQ over this shipment ended.

The phone call was unexpected, and I was baffled by the resolution.

I had never given a second sample to CIQ or Mr. Zeng.

Why Pretzels?

"Why pretzels?" I asked Joe over instant messenger. I hated pretzels. My earliest memory of a pretzel was the little hard brown ones that people ate with sandwiches. When I was younger and new to the US, I distinctly recalled watching my friend choose pretzels over a bag of Doritos.

Why is this fool eating that tasteless crap? I thought back then. Funny how life changes.

It was 9:00 p.m. in Kuwait City in early 2007, and I was only getting started with the data crunching and analysis for a presentation I had to make to a client the following day for my consultancy job. Joe was chatting during his lunchtime from his office in the D.C. area. We had graduated from Wharton over a year ago and I had landed a position with a global strategy consulting firm which took me all over the world. Joe had achieved his goal as well—entering the private equity world in real estate. But we had an itch our corporate jobs could not satisfy—a dream of building and operating a business from the ground up. The week before, I had mentioned my unsuccessful attempt during the previous summer to purchase a fast food franchise in New Jersey. The idea of buying a franchise resonated with Joe, and he had suggested Auntie Anne's. Our goal, however, was not to operate one brand by itself, but to do something much bigger. We intended to build a full back-office infrastructure, from logistics to accounting, which could support our dream of launching a portfolio of brands in the China market.

"Carlie loves Auntie Anne's! Every time we go to the mall, the lines are at least thirty minutes long. Asians make up a good portion of the people in line, so that is a good sign," Joe responded, referring to his wife Carlie.

"I have never had one in my life. I vaguely remember seeing the brand in airports and malls. Have you had it before? Is it that good?" I asked as I looked up Auntie Anne's website. Looking at the logo, I remembered that my soon-to-be wife Karen loved it as well. Like Carlie, she often bought one when we went to malls.

So what was this brand, and why did it ultimately excite us?

Anne of Auntie Anne's Pretzels is Anne Beiler. In 1988, she began mixing, twisting and baking pretzels and a variety of snacks at a farmer's market in Downingtown, Pennsylvania. One day, Anne and her husband Jonas ran out of raw ingredients to make their typical pretzels, so they used the materials they had left in their kitchen. The change in recipe caused their sales to soar. The pretzels sold so well that they decided to stop selling anything else. The recipe they discovered in 1988 is the same recipe sold today at over a thousand stores in over twenty countries.

In addition to the famous pretzel, Auntie Anne's also sold pretzel dogs and lemonade. Through the years, the chain also introduced other minor innovations, such as the Pretzel Pocket, Funnelz, and even pizza. Nonetheless, the menu has revolved primarily around traditional pretzels.

In the US, the stores became extremely popular in most malls and transportation hubs, so it was proven to make money. Another plus: somehow, the brand had taken on a very nostalgic, comforting feeling. Many consumers could often recall a personal experience with Auntie Anne's. Few brands could claim this kind of emotional bond. More amazing was that Auntie Anne's had never invested in any above-the-line advertising (that is, TV, radio, print media, etc.). Their marketing plan was simple: enthusiastic employees offering samples of piping hot pretzels to anyone walking within a few feet of the stores.

In Asia, Auntie Anne's had done extremely well. Walk through the bustling streets of Bangkok, and you would notice a few things. Vast number of street vendors, situated one after another, serving up fragrant, exotic dishes with fresh, flavorful ingredients. The colors of the dishes cover the entire rainbow spectrum. Prices for these foods were cheap by any standard. Now escape from the hot, humid weather into the refreshingly cold air-conditioned malls that were scattered throughout the city. There were still local food options like tom yum soup and pad thai, but there would be a good chance that you would see an Auntie Anne's. With over eighty-five Auntie Anne's stores in the country, it was hard to miss.

Auntie Anne's began its international franchising early, starting with Jakarta, Indonesia, in 1995. By the next year, Auntie Anne's stores were opened in the Philippines, Malaysia, and Singapore. The growth in these different countries continues on a rapid pace even today. The most successful franchisees in Asia were in Thailand (with over eighty-five stores), Korea (with over thirty stores), Malaysia (with around twenty five stores), and Japan (with eight stores in their first year). Along the way, Auntie Anne's learned some key lessons in how to support international franchisees. Many franchisers wanted the brand to be exactly the same abroad as it is the US or Europe, and did not allow for the flexibility to adapt processes and menu items to the local market. Auntie Anne's seemed very supportive in giving flexibility without compromising the core products and image of the brand.

We visited many markets to see with our own eyes why Auntie Anne's succeeded. We wanted to replicate the actions that made these franchisees successful. In Thailand, food is cheap, competition is high, and foreign brands are abundant. Customers are fickle and demanding. Theoretically, Auntie Anne's should not have succeeded there, yet the brand has grown more successful each passing year. Success was due to the fact that the franchisees were not only experienced with operating other food franchises, they also had access to great locations and investment capital. Many stores were launched quickly and the franchisee did an excellent job of updating the menu frequently with seasonal products.

Few international franchises have started out with runaway successes, and Auntie Anne's was no different. Each franchisee took a different path to grow, and most successful franchisees agreed that starting out was not easy. In some cases, it took two or three years and hefty investment, or even five years or more to reach the tipping point in consistent profitability. Even so, we thought this brand could succeed in China. We would face many challenges along the way, but felt that they are all solvable.

Two franchises in Asia that gave us pause were in Taiwan and Hong Kong, as they did not perform near expectations. Although their performance could be attributed to the fact that neither group invested heavily in developing the brand or customizing the product lines to the local market, we were nonetheless worried that they were failing because Chinese people had many more food options than people in other countries—or maybe different taste buds.

Anne ran the firm through the initial growth stages until the early 2000s, when she sold it to her cousin, Sam Beiler. Sam started in the firm as a regional representative, so he knew the business, its products, and its strengths. Instead of focusing on a mixture of self-owned stores and franchises, he shrewdly focused entirely on franchising and sold off the majority of the company-owned stores to pay off the debt he assumed when acquiring the brand. In late 2010, Sam cashed out and sold Auntie Anne's to FOCUS Brands, a private firm that also owned a variety of other brands, including Cinnabon, Carvel, Schlotzsky's, and Moe's Southwestern Grill.

As a business in the US market, Auntie Anne's was quite amazing. The pretzel could sell for as much as four dollars, the price of a Subway six-inch sandwich or a McDonalds Extra Value Meal. The food cost is obviously much less than that of an Extra Value Meal. With that type of price and low food costs, the margins for this business were much higher than those of other franchise concepts. The attractive economics sold Joe on the brand.

Another key point that sold both Joe and I was that as new entrants to this industry, we did not want a brand with complicated operations. Though making a perfect Auntie Anne's pretzel is not easy, the complexity paled compared to the likes of a full service restaurant like McDonalds or KFC. Our thought was that we would start with a snack brand like Auntie Anne's and grow into opening full restaurant brands later. Baby steps, so to say.

In 2007, Joe and I believed in Auntie Anne's. We did so because of the Auntie Anne's team, the performance of the brand in other countries, and the quality of the pretzel itself.

"Yeah, the product is very good. I did not snack too much, but like I mentioned, the lines are always long. I can give them a call to see if franchising abroad is even a possibility," Joe typed. With that, we sealed our involvement with Auntie Anne's Pretzels, a brand that neither Joe nor I were too familiar with.

Forming the
Team and the Plan

Over the next week, I did not think much about pretzels. Discussing business ideas was something I enjoyed doing, and I could go through ten of them in a week. I wanted to engage in an entrepreneurial activity fulltime, but did not have the courage to quit my job and look into doing so.

When I was seven years old, my parents moved the whole family from Taiwan to the US in search of better educational and career opportunities for my siblings and me. After supporting me through undergraduate and graduate degrees, I did not want them to worry about my career choices. Personally, I needed my parents' approval. In order to obtain that approval, I needed to show them that the entrepreneurial activity would not leave me hungry.

A franchise was perfect, because it carried a name brand that serves as a stamp of approval that I could show to my parents. Also, if we were not successful, at least we would have had the achievement of locking down the brand in the first place. I was also adamant that I would not leave my cushy job without a business partner. Solo entrepreneurs and CEOs alike often talked about how lonely and challenging it was to be the key decision maker.

A week later, it looked like I had found both a partner and a franchise. "Good news!" Joe typed. "Auntie Anne's franchise is actually available for China."

"All of China?" I replied, instantly thinking of the bigger picture. For my consulting job, I was currently developing strategy for a franchise that had 20,000 locations worldwide. Because of this work, I knew that China was the holy grail of international expansion for businesses. "That would be amazing if we could take down the brand for all of China. Pretty big deal if we could do it."

"Yes, the entire mainland of China and Macao are available. The lady I talked to from headquarters mentioned that if we were interested, we should submit a business plan quickly. They are currently considering who to award the franchise to. Supposedly, they have a bunch of applicants that they are evaluating. I gave her a quick run-down of our team, and she said that she will recommend that the management keep the process open for us."

"What team? You mean just you and I?" I asked.

"No, I added a few people, including Jonathan and Bill. You do not know Jonathan, but he is a friend from Berkeley. His family runs a chain of Chinese restaurants in the Middle East, so he can be our expert in food. And I included Bill because you said that his family does real estate in China. He will be our local on-the-ground connections guy," Joe replied.

"Of course," he continued. "We need to make sure that they are interested. If not, we can find other people with similar backgrounds to fill in. I needed to present a full team for Auntie Anne's for them to consider us."

"Makes sense," I said. "Well, let me ask Bill to see if he is interested. You think your friend Jonathan would be interested?" Bill lived in Hong Kong at the time, but had told me he had acquired a department store in Beijing, so I thought he might start spending more time there. My thought was that if Bill decided to join, then we could start in his malls.

"Not sure, but I will ask. Jonathan is pretty down for these types of ventures. Most likely, he will be in the background, listed as an investor for the pitch. We would need to operate it ourselves," Joe said.

Over the following few days, Joe and I discussed the opportunity with Jonathan and Bill, and they both joined the group. We then informed Auntie Anne's headquarters that we had a team and would be submitting a business plan in a month or so. They agreed to wait for our submission before awarding the franchise.

Finding Investors

"Wen-Szu, I heard that you are trying to franchise Auntie Anne's Pretzels for China? If you are looking for investors, my friends and I would be interested," Parker wrote in the email. Parker was someone that I had met three years earlier in Dallas. I had not communicated with him since, but somehow he heard through mutual friends about what we wanted to do.

Luckily for us, the economy was on a tear in 2007, so people had ample cash and were looking for places to park their investment dollars. China was already a hot topic, deemed as the site of future growth in the world; the success of KFC and McDonalds there was etched on everyone's mind. During that time, finding investors was easy. Friends and acquaintances were seeking us out to invest.

Like everything else we did, we made a plan and created a criteria list to describe the type of investors we wanted. We turned down many investors, including Parker, because we only wanted someone who could contribute in some way: namely someone strategic, either because they had connections in China or because they could provide a professional service that saved us cash. The plan was to start small, with a few stores to show that the concept worked. Then, we would raise additional rounds of investments.

A few months into the process, we started to feel that Bill might not be as devoted to the concept as we had thought. Although he attended most of our conference calls and gave his opinions here and there, he was increasingly non-committal on investing himself or dedicating his resources and time. As insurance, we decided to find someone else with solid contacts in China. Joe and Jonathan suggested Justin Luo, one of their college friends, because his father was an influential Asian-American figure with many ties to China. Joe approached Justin about the idea, and after a few discussions Justin signed on as our fifth team member. The deal was that Joe and I would run the day-to-day operations while the team members assisted through their connections and areas of expertise.

Justin turned out to be a valuable member of the team, as he helped raise investment dollars from people who had connections in China. This helped make the entire fundraising process very smooth and quick.

The Business Plan

A business plan is a story, one that weaves in bits of information to explain with compelling reasons why the business would be successful. Our challenge was to convince Auntie Anne's corporate why they should award the franchising rights in China to recent MBA graduates with little operations experience. It was exciting. To assemble a compelling business plan, we needed more information than the investor list to convince Auntie Anne's that we were the right team—and ourselves that this was the right opportunity. My franchise-related consulting work required me to travel to several Asian countries where Auntie Anne's had a presence, so I was able to understand how the brand worked in each of the locales. I set up visits with the franchisees of Auntie Anne's stores in Asia. I took copious notes on what they did and how they became successful, and we incorporated their advice into our planning.

Meanwhile, Joe used the information we were gathering to create a financial model, an Excel spreadsheet that projected sales and costs. Joe's model was impressive, and allowed us to see the financial impact on the whole business by adjusting a few variables. For instance, inputting in some information about our expectations, such as how many stores we opened and how many cities we were present in, could show us a full financial picture of how the business would perform. We tried to stay extremely conservative in our estimations and even reduced the lowest sales projections by twenty percent. From the numbers, the business looked extremely promising.

The entire planning process took a bit longer than expected—around two months to finish the fifty-three-page business plan and eighty megabyte financial model. We then submitted the business plan to Auntie Anne's and they quickly invited us to make a presentation at their headquarters.

The Negotiations

During the entire negotiation period with Auntie Anne's, my fiancée, Karen, and I were planning out our wedding, set for late December 2007. Karen and I had dated for years already and I tend to joke about various milestones or cultural differences through this process. Please allow me to draw a parallel between the franchising procedure and the courting process of my fiancée – no offense or sexual discrimination intended, of course.

Let us start with initial impressions. Making a great first impression is crucial in any relationship, and there tends to be over-exaggerations about one's talents and worth. We had a few hours to pitch to Auntie Anne's corporate, so it felt like speed dating. Borrowing a shiny black Mercedes E320 that I could not afford to own, Jonathan, Joe and I dressed up in our sharpest suits and ties and strode into the Auntie Anne's headquarters, armed with a one-hundred slide PowerPoint deck that covered potential questions and our entry strategy.

Auntie Anne's was recognized as one of the top franchisers in the US. Similar to courting a sexy girl who knows she is beautiful, we had preconceived notions that Auntie Anne's corporate would be pretentious and judgmental. We were prepared to walk into something that felt like a Wall Street conference room, but instead entered a world far different from the hard-grinding corporate life to which we were accustomed. Everyone in that rural Pennsylvania town was just so... nice. Warm and genuinely inviting. Before our presentation, the CEO called an all-hands meeting at the cafeteria, where he personally introduced each of us to the entire office, to roaring cheers and applause. It felt like a scene out of the TV show *Friday Night Lights*, when the football coach was motivating the entire school as part of a pep rally. Then everyone, over a hundred people, rushed up for introductions and warm handshakes. Scott, the Chief Customer Officer. Bill, the Chief Operating Officer. Kevin, the Director of Training. Melanie, the Food Scientist. Valerie, the Head of Communication. And on and on. There we were in dark suits and ties, and the majority of the Auntie Anne's crowd was in long sleeve T-shirts and jeans.

Talk about love at first sight. We felt instantly comfortable with everyone we met as they said things like, "Welcome to Auntie Anne's! Come try out these pretzels. Eat yourself full!" Some of them talked to us in what I learned was a Pennsylvania Dutch English accent, which sounded country to me. Growing up in Indiana, I associated country accents with nice, church-going people.

Our direct counterparts in the discussions were Mike McCoy, the Director of International Operations, and John Roda, Legal Counsel and Head of Franchising. Mike was a big fellow, tall and strong with a bald shiny head like Mr. Clean, yet with a warm and caring face that made him more like a big, friendly teddy bear. John had a more serious face, and looked like a professor of literature with his thinly-rimmed glasses, well-pressed khakis, and button-up shirt. Both men were well traveled, and could discuss any foreign topic intelligently, from politics to culture. Mike loved sports and enjoyed chatting about college football or any professional sport. John enjoyed discussing his experiences abroad.

Our "presentation" turned out to be a very friendly, team-oriented discussion about our plans and our thoughts about how to make the brand work in China. The discussion was constructive, almost like a brainstorming session. In fact, the conference room seemed almost too formal for it: we could have been talking over beers or barbeque. We left very positively charged by the opportunity, and by the great support team at Auntie Anne's. We felt that they truly cared about relationships, not just numbers. Though they did not want to give up the full rights to China, we pressed for this as a required condition.

A few weeks later, we received formal notice that we had won the rights for China. Next, we needed to work through the details of the letter of intent (LOI) and master franchise agreement (MFA). Discussing the LOI felt like taking all the serious conversations about a couple's future during the entire dating period and condensing it into a few short discussions. Please indulge me again on the comparison to the courting process[1].

"Can we sub-franchise to other groups?" equated to "How many kids do you want?"

"What cities are you going to open your stores?" meant the same thing as "Where will we live?"

But one question stayed the same. "How much money will you make for us?"

We agreed upon the financial terms of the deal during this stage. A few items in this letter represented the most important aspects of a franchise: initial franchise fees, recurring royalties, term of the contract and rights, exclusivity, included geography of the franchise, and sub-franchise terms.

After three months of discussion, we got engaged to Auntie Anne's and signed the LOI.

---

1   Analogies not intended to offend either gender or cultures but serve as a light hearted entertainment

Anyone who has ever had to plan a wedding would understand the overwhelming amount of details that needed to be covered. Emotions ran high, and all sides tend to fight over insignificant details, with each argument becoming increasingly bitter. Negotiating the terms of an MFA was more emotional and complicated, with details in a technical language I did not understand, and a contract that spanned one hundred and seventy-eight pages. We had to be extremely careful about how it was negotiated.

Fortunately, we had the full support of my best friend from childhood, Faiz Ahmad, through the entire process. Faiz was a lawyer at a top global law firm at that time, and he remains one of the best negotiators I have ever met. When Faiz first enrolled in college, he was so enamored with the freedom of living on campus and hanging out with other people that he rarely went to class. His grades from his first and second year majoring in biology were less than desirable. However, when he became more serious about his academics in his junior year, he decided that he wanted to change majors as well, and here was where his brilliance as a negotiator first appeared. He was able to convince the Dean of Economics to allow him to drop the grades he had received in all of his biology-related classes and change his major to Economics. After the change, he upgraded his grades to a near 4.0 GPA. If we had hired someone else of his caliber to do the negotiating, we would have paid out tens of thousands of dollars for the countless hours that he put in.

For those not familiar with franchises, here is a quick primer. The brand is considered a franchiser (the wife), and people who franchise from the brand are considered franchisees (the husband). A franchiser makes money through initial franchise fees (a dowry), on-going payments of a percentage of the gross sales, called a royalty (costs to maintain minimum living standards for the couple) and a mark-up on ingredients sold to the franchisees (money from a husband's salary to buy presents and vacations to keep the wife happy). Many franchisers would also tack on an extra few percent for an advertising fund to be used by corporate on behalf of all franchisees (things purchased by the wife on behalf of the family, regardless if the husband likes it or not). For instance, advertisements for Subway sandwiches all around the US were paid not by Subway's headquarters, but by the franchisees, under the supervision of the brand's headquarters. Does not matter if the franchisees like Jared the Subway Guy or not, the franchisees are stuck with him.

Typical franchise fees for individual stores in the US ranged between $10,000 and $50,000. For international franchises, franchisees usually tried to buy the rights to a city, region, or in our case, a whole country. Here the franchise fees could range from tens of thousands to millions, depending on the potential size of the market. Often, the fees were back-calculated to see how many stores one could open, and then a discounted franchise fee for each store would be added. For international franchises, the franchisers often set an additional opening fee for each store. This fee is similar to the costs associated with having kids, with each one requiring a certain amount.

Royalties for franchises ranged between two and eight percent. The actual number depended on how strong the brand name was, how big of a player the franchisee was, and how the contract was negotiated. In established markets like US, most franchisers would have a set rate that was non-negotiable. In international markets, it was all negotiable. Too bad that is not the case with the wife.

For international franchisees, exclusivity and geography mattered as well. In our case, we wanted all of China or nothing. We also needed exclusivity, meaning that we would be the only player allowed to open Auntie Anne's in the country. I hope I do not need to spell out how this compares to a marriage. Our growth would be through sub-franchising, meaning that we would act as franchisers to people who wanted to open the brand in China. In the case of sub-franchising, we would share the royalty and franchise fees collected with headquarters, according to a pre-negotiated schedule.

Most brands managed the international franchisees through a development schedule, sort of like a career timeline for the husband. Franchisers obviously wanted their brand to grow in whatever country they enter. The best way to do that was to grow the number of stores. The development schedule was a projection of the number of stores that would be opened in upcoming years. Should the number of stores opened fall short of the development schedule, the franchiser could default on the entire MFA. Should the husband become unemployed or bankrupt, there could be a default on the marriage. In fact, a development schedule is often where most MFAs default, as it is difficult to keep the growth at the same pace as early expectations.

Terms of the contract could range from five years to thirty years or more, depending on how it was negotiated. In the US, the average term was five years for a franchisee, but there was usually a free renewal if the performance is adequate.

The letter of intent covered the key terms listed above. After we signed the LOI with Auntie Anne's, we still took months to go through the MFA. We negotiated the LOI pretty hard and tried to expose holes wherever we could on every point. Through this process, headquarters realized that their current MFA had room to improve, since the contract had not been updated for years. So Auntie Anne's hired an outside consultant to rewrite the contract.

The MFA contained terms and clauses to protect the brand, so most of it was not negotiable. Like a wedding, many items are not negotiable, even if the guy thinks it is. Thou must have flower arrangements. Yes, all family members must be invited. No, exes are not allowed. Nonetheless, we discussed and negotiated every point. This prolonged negotiation surprised and irritated headquarters. Several times they told us that a franchise was a system that was proven and should not and could not be changed. Therefore our negotiations, they said, went against the norm.

The Negotiations

After months of negotiation, hundreds of emails, and many heated conference calls, we finalized the MFA. Planning the wedding took about the same amount of effort. On December 31, 2007, nine days after my wedding, we finally signed the MFA.

Moving to China

Beijing or Shanghai?

"Where are we moving to?" Karen asked when we first won the franchise rights, obviously anxious to know where we would begin our lives together.

My answer inspired confidence.

"I have no clue."

The first big decision as an entrepreneur was not an easy one to make. The only real cities we considered for our franchise were Beijing or Shanghai. Of course, there are hundreds of other big cities in China, but our research showed that most firms start in one of these two cities. Before we moved, we sought advice from everyone we talked to. We even visited both cities, and met up with friends who had moved to China years earlier, in order to understand the situation better. The more people we talked to, the more confused I became.

Here is a recap of a conversation at a group dinner in Shanghai, where we listened to the advice of others who were more familiar with China.

"People in the north [Beijing is in the North and Shanghai in the South] eat more noodles and dough-based products, so they will be more accepting of the pretzel," Cindy said. Cindy grew up in Taiwan and her family runs a chain of restaurants in Shanghai, so she seemed like a good source.

"That logic doesn't make sense. People in the north eat more noodles and dough-based products, so opening here will mean that you will have a lot of competition. So, you should go somewhere where there are fewer dough-based options. Open in Shanghai," Adam argued. Adam had been looking at doing some food and beverage investments in both Beijing and Shanghai, and had been researching the industry for quite some time.

"I do not agree. Regardless, there are so many other reasons to start in Beijing. It is the capital so it will carry more significance. Real estate prices are cheaper, fewer foreign competitors than in Shanghai, and you will get the extra benefit of having the Olympics to help you launch the brand. Open in Beijing," Cindy defended.

"Ok. The Olympics reason makes sense, but the others are not good reasons. Registration and other paperwork will be more difficult in Beijing. Rent prices are cheaper for a reason, because the traffic is not as high for the target audience you are going after. Fewer foreign brands mean that locals will not be as accepting of a new foreign brand as in Shanghai. You should start in Shanghai." Adam replied. And so on.

This example was only a small sample. We received an overwhelming volume of advice from everyone, solicited and unsolicited.

In the end, we chose Beijing for two reasons. First, we were entering China around 2008, so the Beijing Olympics were at the top of everyone's mind. According to Auntie Anne's headquarters, this was a good time for retailers because the Olympic city opens itself to the world. Not only does the traffic increase significantly during events like these, the media coverage increases as well. The Olympics in Atlanta proved to be extremely lucrative for the Auntie Anne's franchisees there.

Second—and this was our main reason—we wanted the support of our partner Bill to kick things off. Bill's acquisition of the department store in Beijing had given us confidence that he could provide initial tactical support. Unfortunately, we learned a hard lesson here. During the negotiations, Bill became less and less committal. He started using various reasons, including the excuse that cash was tight. I even offered to loan him the initial investment funds, not knowing that his family was extremely wealthy. I wish he had been upfront about not wanting to join, rather than leading us on with false expectations of support, though perhaps my own assumptions about his interest were to blame. In any case, Bill never did formally decline to be part of the group; he stopped answering our calls and emails. We had moved all the way around the world on the assumption that we would receive initial support from him. But we were deserted.

Getting Settled in Beijing

As I pushed opened the door to my new apartment in Beijing, I was greeted by business card-sized color advertisements and paper flyers jammed in the crack between the door and the door frame. The little cards were cheaply printed with pictures of young girls revealing ample skin and advertising at-home "massage" services. The flyers themselves marketed a range of products and services, including menus and satellite TV. Someone was diligent enough to bypass the security guards at the entrance and stuff my door full of these cards and advertisements every day, which served as a constant reminder for me to lock my doors.

I was so excited about getting the business started that I had overlooked one simple fact: I was moving to Beijing. As a tourist, I had observed and appreciated the cultural differences between Beijing and the US, but as a new resident of the city, I now tried to filter out the "noise" of my new lifestyle. Karen and I decided that after our wedding and honeymoon, I would move to Beijing first, and she would follow when she had a chance to transfer through her firm. Joe and his wife Carlie had made the move together, and arrived a few weeks before I did.

After introducing me to my new apartment on my first day in Beijing, Joe took me to run some critical errands, common for most expats in their first few days. First things first, Joe took me to the police department to register, like a criminal checking in with his parole officer.

"Ha-lo," I greeted the police officer in Chinese as I handed over my passport and my housing lease. Each non-Beijing resident, foreigner and Chinese citizen from another area had to register their whereabouts within three days at the local police station or face fines and deportation.

"What are you doing in China?" the police officer asked nonchalantly as he flipped through my passport in search of my visa. Officially, I was there on a three months tourist visa, so I had to stretch the truth. As he looked through my papers, I was nervous that the police officer would somehow discover my intent to work in China and boot me out of the country. Silly thoughts, I know, but we had heard of other people running into visa issues. A work visa was not easy to obtain, although I had never tried to get one.

"Here you go," he said as he lazily handed back my things, along with official temporary documentation. Surprisingly, the police officer hardly seemed to care. He was just going through the motions of filling in data and printing up the documentation.

"Next!" he called as he cast a worried look at the long line behind me. Amazing! I thought. Something had gone smoothly and easily in China.

Working visas proved difficult for many foreign entrepreneurs in China to obtain. Many people used 3rd party visa services that paid local companies to "hire" the foreign entrepreneurs on paper for the visa applications. These services were expensive and a source of constant stress. I was lucky. Although I am an US citizen, the fact that I was born in Taiwan allowed me to obtain a Taiwanese ID. The ID allowed me to enter and stay in China with a very simple application process.

And then we went to open a bank account.

"May I help you?" The bank hostess greeted me, wearing a skirt suit and standing next to a touchscreen kiosk as Joe and I entered the packed lobby.

"I would like to open an account," I said. The employee pressed one of the three buttons on the touchscreen kiosk, and it printed a small sheet of paper bearing the number 141. I looked up at the neon plates above each stall to find the nearest number to mine. The last number was 133. Not bad, I thought. Only two turnovers per teller, given that there were five tellers, so I would have to wait for twenty minutes, max.

"Please take a seat," the hostess told us, but there were no seats left. I studied the neon numbers on top of each teller again, and realized that three of the signs had four-digit numbers, which I would later learn meant they were only reserved for VIPs. So, only two out of the five tellers were reserved for regular or new customers. We stood for close to an hour before my number was called.

As I sat down at the window, the teller stared at me with disdain for a few seconds. I decided to open the conversation.

"Can I open an account?" I asked cautiously, as I placed my passport and a stack of USD into the metal bin connecting us between the thick, bulletproof glass.

"What (something) and (something) do you want?" Her voice cracked over the worn-out mini-speakers, which were the only way for us to hear each other through the glass.

"Excuse me? Can you repeat that?"

"What type of (something) account and (something) do you want!?" she screamed at me through the broken connection. My lack of vocabulary for banking and her lack of patience complicated the process, and everything had to be repeated multiple times. The ensuing conversation was incredibly frustrating as we yelled back and forth at each other for the next forty-five minutes. We filled out close to ten forms that had to be chopped (marked with stamps that act like signatures) by multiple people. She had to help me fill out the forms since I could not write well in Chinese. Her face turned sourer each time I asked for help.

After we left, I thought that I was unlucky, that perhaps I had simply been assigned to someone with a bad attitude. Joe mentioned that he had to wait a long time to open an account as well. Yet, for the next year in China, almost every visit to the bank resulted in the same screaming match, no matter who the employee was. The process itself was emotionally draining and time-consuming. I learned to bring a book with me to the bank, and only go when I felt relaxed and patient.

After the visit to the police station and bank, Joe helped me get settled with a final task for the day. We went to the common pilgrimage destination: Carrefour. This hypermarket was arguably the most successful of its category in China, and often served as a first stop for newcomers to fill their apartments with basic necessities like soap, sheets, and cleaning supplies. Carrying bags of household items home, I noticed the eclectic things that street vendors were selling. An old lady was peddling a small basket of fresh goose eggs. Where did she get fresh goose eggs to sell? Next to her was a man with an entire DVD collection well-packed in his rolling suitcase. If authorities showed up, he could simply zip up and roll his business away. To his right was a typical street vendor setup, consisting of kids' toys laid out over a bed sheet on the ground. At the end of the small row of street vendors, one person displayed three tiny puppies snuggling together for body warmth. The puppies were barely the size of my hand and incredibly cute, but looked too young to be separated from their mother.

Several realizations dawned on me that first day in Beijing. First, this was a very large city. The streets often had six to seven lanes—in each direction! The "local" police station where I had gone to register myself was ten minutes away by car. Ten minutes by car in Beijing was not like ten minutes in the suburbs of America, where one was on a highway driving past wide retail plazas with ample parking. Ten minutes by car in Beijing meant passing at least five mega-communities, which were multi-building complexes jam-packed with high-rise apartments and people. Tens of thousands of people. Most communities included a common area with a playground and walking areas, and had five to ten buildings, each anywhere from ten to thirty floors tall. Chinese people are very superstitious and do not have floors for any "unlucky" numbers—that is, no numbers that include the number four (e.g., fourteen, twenty four, etc.) since "four" sounds like the word "death" in Chinese. No number thirteen either, as the country has adopted Western superstitions about unlucky thirteen. So, a building that shows fifteen floors on the floor plans physically only has twelve floors.

Second, the city was gray. Layers of gray smoke blanketed any large building, the product of the daily pollution that eventually caused me to have a sinus operation a few years later. The pollution in China has been well-documented in the news, and the pollution indexes there are considered off the charts by US and European standards. The closest comparison to breathing Beijing air on a polluted day was to find a book with years of dust layered on top. Wipe the dust off as fast as possible so that the grayish particles floated in the air. Lean in and take a big breath. Experience the air of Beijing.

The first few weeks were definitely an adjustment period to the basics of living in Beijing. The streets of Beijing were not dirty per se, as cleaning people come by each day. But I often smelled dried urine and other bodily wastes lurking around in random spots. With so many people and so few public bathrooms, it was not uncommon for taxi drivers and others to relieve themselves against walls. Many toddlers did not use diapers, but instead wear cute little outfits with not so cute slits that run down from the belly button and up the buttocks area. When the kids squatted, the buttocks area opened, leaving a perfect space for them to relieve themselves. Parents did not hesitate to allow their kids to pee or poop on the street. Taxi drivers did not like to pick up passengers with babies in fear that the baby would leave a present. Very efficient for the parents, though.

Beijing is a metropolitan city, as advanced as any in the world, but it definitely has its own personality. With so many people on the streets, drivers had to take a more aggressive attitude or else get stuck behind pedestrians every few meters. For the most part, right-of-way was reserved for whoever is bigger—a true case of nature at work. Cars let buses and trucks pass, bikes let cars pass, and pedestrians learned to scramble for dear life. During my first week in Beijing, I saw a guy walking across a pedestrian crosswalk. He had the right-of-way, but not according to a small truck rushing to take a left turn before the oncoming traffic reached the intersection.

Bam! Though the poor guy did not see the truck, he definitely felt it for weeks to come. The front grill of the tiny truck lifted him off the ground and flung him sideways, where he somersaulted awkwardly and repeatedly for ten feet. His shoulder landed first, then head, then hips, then feet, and then shoulder again. Walking five feet behind him and talking on my mobile phone, I heard a crack and then a raw, deep scream. The best football tackle in the NFL could not have reproduced the impact or violence.

As for the driver, he frantically hopped out of his truck and sprinted around to the front of the truck. Incredibly, he was not concerned about the bleeding man a few feet away, but the grill of his vehicle. No pedestrians approached to help the guy on the ground either, though there were plenty of people who stopped and watched. Following the herd mentality, I stood there and stared, but did not want to get involved unless the person needed immediate medical assistance. Luckily, the injured man survived and walked away with only a fractured arm. After that, like a first grader, I learned to look right and left before walking across any streets, and never talk on a mobile phone when crossing.

When it came to lifestyle, going out to bars required the most adjustment. I enjoy a good mixed drink here and there, and never in my imagination did I think that there would be so much fake alcohol served in Beijing. By fake, I do not mean some dangerous chemistry project used to replace alcohol, but cheaply-made booze poured into the bottles of name brand liquors. Jack Daniels has a very distinct flavor that I look for, one that is hard to mimic. In Beijing, I often tasted that flavor followed by a horrible bitter aftertaste. Alcohol that tastes like this is faked by mixing the real brand with other cheap whiskey. Rumor has it that more Johnny Walker is sold in China than produced worldwide. Before I figured out which bars were honest and which ones were not, I had many mornings with unimaginable hangovers, often from just a few drinks. Needless to say, I learned to watch what I consumed.

The bureaucracies of everyday living proved most difficult to adapt to. When having to wait more than a few minutes in line for anything became painful, I realized I had taken the efficiencies of the US for granted. In China, waiting in line was a typical process for pretty much everything. Paying for electricity and water required using a prepaid card, which was a great financial control tool for the utilities firm. I had to go to the designated banks or locations to charge the card, a process that could easily take over an hour. Worse yet, I often had to go to different locations for each utility. Over the years, I had electricity turned off in the middle of night, as well as hot water and other basic necessities. I learned to watch the meter very closely.

Adjusting to the Beijing lifestyle was difficult, but little did I know the nightmare awaiting us as we tried to register our first store.

Drip 2

The Registration marathon

"Cha Bu Duo (Good Enough)"

October 2007 – January 2008

Like most companies that want to enter China, we started our research by talking to others and through hours of research on Google. The first goal was how to register a company. The information online was limited and processes varied, but it looked very straightforward. Simple flow charts showed a fast, smooth process through each bureau for the business and health license.

We reached out to friends who had done business in China before and asked for advice and referrals. One of the first people who responded was a close friend from college who lived in Los Angeles but traveled to China occasionally, Henry. Though it had been a few years since we had hung out with one another, I still considered Henry a close friend.

"I have registered entities in China before and am familiar with the WFOE (wholly foreign owned entity) registration process," Henry explained over email. "It is a long, confusing process. Do not worry. I have the experience to navigate you through it all."

"Do you have any specific experience with food and beverage firms? From what I have read, it seems like that it involves different bureaus for approvals," I asked.

"My experiences are with registering firms in other industries, but the process for food and beverage could not be that different. I can help you through it for sure," Henry responded. "By the way, the experience that I am bringing to the table is something that has taken me a long time to learn. I will need to charge for it."

"If you are solely responsible for the successful registration of the firm, we can definitely pay you for the services," I offered. "How much are you charging?"

"Well, I will help you find agents to do the paperwork, and can consult you through the process. But I cannot be responsible for the success of it, as there are so many obstacles that could come in the way of it. I am a consultant on this matter," Henry replied.

What we wanted was a person in charge of registering the company, so that Joe and I did not have to worry about it. Henry said that he would give advice but have zero responsibilities on the results of his advice. To top it off, he would not lift a finger to help register the business; we had to hire another firm to do the paperwork. *Would not the firm that we hire through Henry's connection know the process of how to register a WFOE?* I thought. If that was the case, would Henry's only value be that he would refer us to the firm?

"In terms of charges, this is very valuable information and I will save you a lot of time in the complexities of it. Considering that we have known each other for a while, I will only charge $25, 000 USD to consult you through the process," Henry wrote.

"Would you consider equity?" I asked.

"That one is tough. Yes, I think that I could take equity, but since it is more risky, I will need to have at least $75,000-worth in equity," he responded.

Henry lived in LA and had never lived in China before. He had experience in commissioning other firms to register entities for his employer. He had no experience in registering a food and beverage company, and without knowing the details made the assumption that our registration process could not be that different. He was not going to do any paperwork himself. He would not be responsible for the results. He was going to give us the 'friend' discount rate of $25,000 USD upfront.

Was he joking? I had been a management consultant for years and know plenty of corporate lawyers, and I had not heard such outrageous terms. For obvious reasons, we did not hire Henry. But it did give us our first taste of our future business dealings in China; we saw, for the first time, how everyone wanted a piece of us.

January 2008 - February 2008

One common phrase that represented the general attitude of many local Chinese was the concept of "good enough." In Chinese, the phrase is "cha bu duo" literally means "not much difference," although the meaning is closer to "good enough" in English. This term could be applied to all sorts of situations. Ask for a latte but get a cappuccino? Well, "cha bu duo." Ask a printing company to correctly spell your name on a business card, but they still print it wrong anyhow? "Cha bu duo." Ask for a vegetarian meal but still get bits of ground meat in the dish? "Cha bu duo." The excuse got tiring very quickly, but in 2008, it was part of common life in China, professionally and personally.

"Cha bu duo" was not an attitude easily acceptable for some-one who demanded precision and quality like we did. As one of my friends here elegantly phrased it, "cha bu duo my ass, I need this to be perfect."

When it came to legal work and firm registration, "good enough" should not be good enough. Yet we learned that the attitude applied even to legal work. Local agents in China were people who could be hired to help organize the paperwork and get it approved by authorities. Many of these agents had their own specialties; some only dealt with a certain bureau or only certain types of firms (foreign-owned, local, etc.), or certain districts. Though we did not know it at the time, there existed within the system different breeds of local agents aside from their spe-cialties. They could be put into four categories:

Uneducated, no relationships: This category of agents repre-sented a large portion of people marketing themselves as agents. They have minimal education, but a lot of time to wait in line at the bureaus. They have learned the trade as apprentices to other agents. They are usually not from Beijing and have not been in the industry for too long, so they have no relationships to help facilitate the process. This group could help a client get through the process quickly, but the client would always be wondering what they actually registered for, or if the paper-work had been filled out correctly.

Educated, no relationships: This group of agents consisted of peo-ple who have worked in professional settings before and who may even have an office. They know the regulations and rules as defined by the government. Too bad most government-issued rules were not widely published. And even if they were made public knowledge, the "rules" were vague and subject to interpretation by whoever was enforcing them that day. This group is a good source of information and will charge a good premium for their services. Unfortunately, it takes an exasperating amount of time for their work to show any real results.

Uneducated, relationships: The key in China to getting anything passed is having relationships with government bureau employees. There existed within the system agents with no education, and the people they know inside the bureaus defined their jobs. Usually, an agent in this group was from the same province or city as their key contacts. This fact establishes the foundation of trust when gifts needed to be given.

Unfortunately, these agents lived and died by their inside contacts. To win business, many agents tend to overpromise what the government employees can deliver. As a result, the agents themselves are often undependable, as they were in no actual position to fulfill their promises.

Educated, relationships: These agents were rare, as they could usually do better financially with employment in a larger firm or as head of the government bureau division. Almost all mid-sized to large-sized firms has a Government Relations Department. The department is usually headed by someone from a connected family in the government, or an ex-government employee. Running registration for small firms is, quite simply, not worth the hassle for this category of people.

Sadly for us, our foray into the land of the local agents resulted in us finding agents from the first category. Our initial attempts at hiring international law firms were thwarted when they recommended that we hire local agents, since that type of work was too low-level for them. We talked to several referrals from friends and selected one we felt was most honest. We decided on a local agent named Mr. Li.

"Mr. Li."

"The paperwork is in order. Please sign below where I have marked on the documents," Mr. Li said as he pointed to certain sections of the paperwork in front of Joe and me.

We were sitting around Joe's small, round dining table, a location we used as command central in talking to agents and suppliers. Mr.

Li's face was expressionless, but then again, he never showed emotions. He had a skill of maintaining the same facial expression when telling us good or bad news. Indifference was probably a better word to describe his attitude. To say that Mr. Li was a white-collar employee would be a stretch, and one based on pure appearance, though he wore all of the items required to be listed as one. His face was on the long side, and a color that was dark for a Chinese person, probably due to the amount of time he spent outdoors travelling between bureaus. His hair sprouted from the top of his head, with no discernible attempt at combing or styling. Despite a wardrobe of pants and button-down shirts, the overall effect of his appearance was far from professional.

"Hold on a minute," I replied, confused. "What do you mean that the application is ready? You said a few minutes ago that we were missing some initial approvals from the State Administration of Industry and Commerce (SAIC). You said that if we did not have the approvals, we could not move on to the next step." SAIC is the authority in China that approved and granted business licenses and registration. All businesses, local and foreign, needed the final certificate of approval from SAIC prior to opening a business.

"Cha bu duo," Mr. Li suggested. "Let's just submit what we have and see how it goes." I should mention here that Mr. Li was paid the same regardless whether our paperwork passed or not, as his daily job was to go back and forth from clients to the bureaus.

Mr. Li was constantly going to different bureaus and coming back with some type of approved paperwork. His constant activities made the process seem smooth. Mr. Li started as a runner for another agent, responsible for delivering documents back and forth and occasionally standing in line. He learned on the job watching other people, and was promoted to handle his own cases. The initial steps, such as forming the company name for approval, were very straightforward and we understood that process in its entirety. However, over the past week, things had started to go off track.

"What do you mean?" I demanded. "You said that we would not pass if we did not have that documentation. We already failed once for this same reason! Why are you changing your mind now? Do we or do we not need the approvals from the SAIC?"

"No, we do not need it. Please sign and let's move forward," Mr. Li responded patiently. He sounded confident, and wore his usual blank expression.

"If we do not have the approvals, is there a good chance that we will get rejected again?" I pressed. "We have already wasted a week on this part. You told us from the beginning that the entire process would only take a few weeks. We are way behind schedule, and if we keep going on like this, we will not be able to get our license in time. Please be sure. We signed our lease based on the timeline you provided us. We cannot afford to waste any more time, okay?"

Joe and I both picked up our pens, ready to make up for our lost time. My hope was that we did not need more documentation, and I knew I had to confirm my hope with Mr. Li one last time before we signed. Instead, I watched as he stared at the paper in front of us.

"Yes, we need the approvals," Mr. Li blurted out unexpectedly, with the same blank expression.

"F*%#!" I yelled in English.

I was struck with a sudden urge to choke someone. Instead, I shook my head as I leaned my forehead on my palm.

"Make up your mind!" I urged. "Do we sign or not?"

All of our conversations with Mr. Li had been similar to this one: fickle instructions that changed on a dime, the only explanation that of "cha bu duo." After discussions with multiple agents, we realized they all took different processes for the supposedly standardized method of registering a firm.

"Please sign the documents—we do not need the approvals." Mr. Li changed his mind again, probably to shut us up. "I will submit the documents today."

After we signed the paperwork, Mr. Li, in his nonchalant way, excused himself and left.

The paperwork was rejected.

Mr. Li then figured out the issue on why this paperwork was and continued registration. Managing a precise timeline on this process was a nightmare and impossible. The discombobulated task of registering our business involved numerous approvals and paperwork from different bureaus to assemble the complete package of documents required for the full application.

Mr. Li was supposed to get these documents ready in less than two weeks. That process was delayed for over five weeks. Throughout, we learned nothing definitive about the process, only random bits of conflicting information Mr. Li offered. Adding to our frustration was the realization that the approvals Mr. Li was chasing were not covered in the high-level instructions, issued by the government, on how to register a company.

Many government employees were paid at most a few hundred US dollars per month, yet their decisions on licensing and enforcement could save or cost companies millions. This unbalanced equation led to an obvious incentive for firms to give gifts, and create a culture where government employees demanded them.

China was making effort to crack down on the graft. Everyone knew that the hunt was on. Did it stop the bribes or gift-giving from happening? No. The format of how it was done simply changed. Now, most government employees would only take gifts from people they could trust. Finding a relationship channel that led back to a government employee became a key action item for companies. Otherwise, one needed to invest a lot of time in building up the trust of a government employee to get them to accept anything.

Incredibly, this system powered by relationships, or guanxi, was still faster than any "published" processes. Given our Western upbringing, we had a difficult time believing the significance of relationships in this culture. Rather, we sought after a more reputable stamp of approval on our process. After Mr. Li took five weeks to prepare the full application, we mistakenly let a more "professional" firm review the documents before submitting.

Getting Fired
By Our Lawyer

February 2008 – May 2008

Jackson Smith was an odd character. He started the law firm Smith and Yuan with a local Chinese lawyer in early 2000's. In China, foreign lawyers were not allowed to formally practice, as they were not allowed to take the local bar exam. Despite that, Jackson was one of the self-proclaimed exceptions, as he stated that he was the only foreign lawyer listed as a member of the bar association in China.

Part of what we learned about the firm came from an online ad, which stated that the firm specialized in registering and shutting down representative offices and WFOEs for foreign firms. They also performed the full range of accounting and tax filing services for companies and individuals. The ad mentioned that they could reduce the hassle for local compliance, which to me meant that they are familiar with navigating local laws and compliance issues. The ad listed the key competencies that we needed.

The firm had more than fifty lawyers in 2008, yet the structure was different from other integrated firms. Jackson handled his own work with only one associate. The rest of the law firm was run by his partner, Yuan, in a separate office. Except for the shared name and marketing efforts, the firm seemed like two separate entities.

Still, we were interested in Smith and Yuan, because they claimed to be experts in franchising and in the food and beverage industry. We were thrilled at the credentials—and the fact that they spoke English.

Jackson had lived in China for close to 30 years, as he was one of the first Americans invited here after Deng Xiaoping opened China's doors to the West. Jackson's background was impressive, with a law degree from an Ivy League school and a recipient of a prestigious international scholarship. He spoke Chinese well, almost fluently, but still carried a noticeable accent that gave away his foreign upbringing. Strangely, his "American" English also carried an accent, though it was hard to pinpoint. Jackson was Caucasian, a little under six feet tall and slender, with thin-rimmed glasses and flat, oily hair pasted from the left to the right side of his head. His social etiquette was not that of a local Chinese, yet not that of an American. The timing of his gaze, his manner of speech, and method of movement were all slightly off (relative to both cultures), to the point of being awkward. He was quiet by nature and seemed like an intellectual with his prolonged, pensive stares and demeanor. On the several occasions I went into his office, I usually found him staring out of the window, seemingly thinking and reflecting.

Jackson was married with kids. Jessica, his Chinese wife, worked with him. She ran a separate accounting firm that augmented his services as a law firm, but together it looked like two departments in the same firm. While Jackson had a large office with a beautiful window view of the rest of the central business district, Jessica had a small cubicle outside his office next to the other secretaries. Jessica seemed like an obedient wife, always nodding her head at every word from Jackson's mouth. In reality, she seemed more scared than obedient. Several times, when his temper flared up, she cowered away and disappeared quickly from sight.

Smith and Yuan was referred to us by an Italian entrepreneur who was trying to set up a gelato franchise. In late February 2008, we took the final set of paperwork prepared by our local agent, Mr. Li, to Jackson for a final check before we submitted. Jackson assigned the work to his only associate, Steven Ling.

Steven was a Chinese lawyer who had been working with Jackson for the past few years. He was around five-feet, eight-inches tall, with a strong thick build and a rectangular, chiseled face. Hard-working and honest, Steven's method of speaking and his approach with people made him seem very dependable. He was married with one daughter, so the source of his motivation and work ethic was supporting his family. Steven served as a prosecutor in another province, which explained his strict moral code, which we loved.

The day after we submitted the paperwork for the firms review, we met in their office to discuss it.

"Your paperwork was filled out completely incorrect," Jackson sternly warned. "Did you know that you are registering your firm in Shanghai and not Beijing?"

"What do you mean? Our agent mentioned that the paperwork is pretty standard and that we were registering the firm in Beijing," I defended, knowing that they were going to prove me wrong.

"It is not the case here. Let Steven show you," Jackson explained, as he had Steven show us where the paperwork read "Pudong, Shanghai" rather than "Beijing."

How was that possible? I asked myself. I could overlook details at times, but this is like going out to buy diapers and coming home with a six-pack of beer. Talk about feeling stupid.

We were upset, to say the least, that we had missed this major issue. We were quickly losing confidence in Mr. Li, and Jackson was making a good case as to why we needed other professional consultation.

"Do you have experience in this area?" we asked our newfound legal team.

"Yes, we have plenty of experience in registering companies in the food industry," Jackson assured us. "In fact, we recently successfully registered licenses with the health bureau and all bureaus relating to the food industry. Your case is typical of the cases that we have registered before."

"I must be upfront to state that we do not have any inside 'guanxi' in any of the bureaus, but that we follow the law and register for every license by the book," he told us then.

"It's great that you do it that way, since that is how we want to operate," I said.

Jackson's openness made us feel confident that he would not jeopardize our moral code for a shortcut.

"We want to work with professionals who have experience and who can guide us through this entire process without a hitch," I said. "Can you give us a breakdown of the timeline?"

Jackson explained the high-level timelines involved in obtaining the licenses from the health bureau, environmental bureau, and the various business bureaus. He then asked Steven to give us the details on how long each process would take.

Steven proceeded to explain the bureau-issued dates required for each step. Our hopes rose once again. Despite Mr. Li's crappy work, our duo of lawyers sounded professional and experienced. They gave us the full assurance that they could complete the process for us before our scheduled opening in June. Past the point of frustration with Mr. Li, we decided on the spot to move all of our registration work to Smith and Yuan.

We were upfront with Jackson about our goals for Chinese operations of Auntie Anne's: we wanted to build a franchise business after launching several stores on our own. We told them we had already found our first location at the Gate Mall and wanted to open before the Olympics.

"How sure are you of the timeline?" we asked again.

"The full registration should take no more than two months. Your case is very standard and we should not have issues with the process," Jackson said confidently.

We immediately began working with them to update our first set of paperwork for the Ministry of Commerce (MOFCOM), the bureau that manages foreign corporations. They changed our registration from a restaurant management firm to a restaurant company with Gate Mall as our headquarters.

Unfortunately, our excitement over finding a new ally did not last long. Problems and delays started to show up immediately. Over the next few weeks, we worked closely through each step of the registration process. Each time we met up to discuss our status there were hiccups in the timeline they had originally presented to us. The timeline was pushed back repeatedly, and over small issues they seemed confused about.

They quoted us official timelines from websites, but in China, unless one had guanxi, nothing ever happens on schedule. The official websites also lacked details about required documentation that took time to obtain. As we had already seen, any front desk employee could delay a business by simply claiming that the paperwork was filled out incorrectly, regardless of whether or not it was. Each time we met with our new agents, we pressed Jackson for more accurate timeline and information. Tensions were rising on both sides.

Meanwhile, we engaged Jessica's firm to help us with our accounting. We discussed our situation with her and she prepared a professional, detailed quote for us. We were happy to include her and her firm, and wanted to use her services on a regular basis.

During our initial dealings with him, Jackson's true personality reared its head a few times. Once we were discussing Steven's approach on the first set of MOFCOM registration documents—an approach which led to the process being delayed by a week or more. We loved Steven and his attitude at this point, yet we were visibly upset at the unexpected delays and lack of communication on their part.

Jackson must have seen our conversations with him as accusatory.

"Jackson, the delay was unfortunate, but the process needs to be managed better and more accurately," Joe told him one day. "But, please, please, do not be mad at Steven."

Jackson was quiet throughout the conversation, listening to our complaints and questions. After about ten minutes, he motioned for us to be quiet.

"I..." Jackson pressed his lips together tightly and pointed towards us with his right index finger. His left hand was balled up into a fist. "I..."

Jackson wiggled his index finger towards us again. His lips were turning white and were still tightly pinned together, and he was now shaking his head right to left ever so slightly.

"I would take Steven as an employee over ten of you!!" Jackson screeched at last. He gave us a glare of pure, unexpected hatred. "Don't you dare walk in here and accuse us of not finishing our work on time! These delays are caused by the government and not us!"

Jackson's anger was passionate and sudden. Surprisingly, it triggered the exact same fury in Joe. Joe was always professional and respectful when dealing with elders and other professionals. His words were well-thought out and logical, and he hardly ever lost his cool in formal discussions such as these. Yet, Jackson's delivery touched a nerve in Joe, who never stood for disrespect of any kind.

"Jackson! Mr. Smith! Let's go to your office and talk! Now!" Joe said with authority.

He then stood up to hold open the door and waved his hand, signaling for Jackson to follow. Jackson must have been doubly surprised by Joe's change in demeanor, because he stood up. For a few seconds that felt like eternity for me, they stared each other down. Finally, Joe broke the silence.

"Let's talk in your office. Now, please!" Joe insisted.

I sat there stunned, alone in the conference room. Jackson's glass office was right down the hall, and I had a perfect seat for the entertainment about to ensue. Watching two people face off behind a glass wall was like viewing a silent movie, only without the dramatic soundtrack. This silent movie had plenty of gesticulations, back and forth pacing, fast talking on both Joe and Jackson's part. At one point, Jackson took a seat and began to look quieter and calmer, but further observation revealed that he was still steaming at the collar. I was surprised that they did not start swinging at each other.

Eventually, Joe eased his pace and gestures but continued to talk. It was reminiscent of a parent talking a child down from a tantrum. They continued for about ten to fifteen minutes before they both walked back into the conference room, civilized and calm. Joe even cracked a joke to lighten the mood. They could have hugged at this point.

Joe recalled later that he was pissed off at the undeserved, disrespectful outburst from Jackson, and his manner of communication. They agreed that we should all discuss the issues as a group, and that we were working on the same side.

Though we were able to overcome the challenges of that day, the issues with registration continued. Again and again, we ran into situations where we were delayed in an unpredictable fashion. After a few weeks, we had moved past several bureaus, but were stuck at the health bureau, which said our location did not qualify for baking on-site, though Jackson had earlier assured us that doing so would be no problem.

The tension climaxed dramatically when we saw the bill.

The bill that the firm submitted to us was outrageous. The invoice included time spent conducting research in areas that they claimed to be experts in when they first solicited our business.

Joe, being the finance- and detail-oriented person he was, audited the bill thoroughly. We then sat down with Jackson to discuss it. Joe reviewed each line item and started to cross some things out, reducing the hours. Four hours of standing in line? Yeah, right. One. Eight hours of online research into laws they said they knew? Do not think so. Zero. And so on.

As Joe went down the list, Jackson sat calmly back in his chair and listened to everything. In hindsight, I realized that he was repeating actions from his previous outburst—gripping his hands together in front of him to the point that they started turning white.

When Joe finished, Jackson said in a very quiet, controlled voice that we could choose to pay or not pay the bill. However, he would resign as our lawyer, effective immediately. We were speechless.

In a less calm voice, he then told us that his wife's accounting firm would also no longer do business with us.

And when Joe once again tried, very methodically and logically, to explain why the costs should be lower than what they were, Jackson blew up. Again.

"In all my years of law, no one has ever tried to negotiate or challenge the billing statement," he said.

"Jackson," I said in a low, soothing voice, hoping to calm him down. "We have paid your rates before, so the bill rates are not the issue here. The issue is that fact that we were charged for research time. We hired your firm because you claimed to be experts in registration for the food and beverage industry. Why would you need to spend dozens of hours reading up on the laws and regulations? If I were an expert on the industry, even if there are constant changes to the laws, it would be my responsibility to know it."

"Let me give you an example," I continued. "My background is in information technology. We installed Microsoft Windows for our clients. Did I charge them for the time I spent reading and learning how to do that? Of course not. Our clients paid us for our expertise, and we charged for only the time that we spent installing. This is why we do not understand how you can charge us for learning a subject that you are a supposedly an expert in."

I felt pretty clever to think up that analogy on the spot. But Jackson was not exactly amused. He shrugged off my comments and turned his head to signal the secretary, asking her to find Steven. Awkward silence blanketed the room as we waited.

"Steven," Jackson said as Steven cautiously entered the room, apparently sensing the tension. "Please prepare all of their materials and return it to them as soon as you can." With that, Jackson stood up and walked out of the room.

Though Jackson said we did not have to pay the bill, we did what we thought was right and paid the amount that we thought was fair.

Below is an email from Jackson we received later that day, to officially resign as our lawyer.

Dear Joe and Wen-Szu:

I appreciate the effort you are putting into your project. You need the best professional advice and that is what we are giving you. You also need to be prepared to pay for it. As you continue to get more experience in business and life, you will come to realize it's always best to be "da fang", loosely translated as generous, rather than penny-pinching in your dealings with people. In particular, you need good professional partners. One of my clients last year, on receiving an invoice, immediately wired twice the amount of the invoice to us because he was so grateful at the quality of the work he was getting. You are different.

Lawyers sell time. If you want a lawyer to accompany you to do this or that, you pay for the time at lawyers' rates. It's that simple. The comments you inserted on the invoice reveal that you are trying to get something for nothing. People who operate that way rarely succeed in China - or anywhere.

Go ahead and pay the [money]. We resign as your law firm. Smith & Yuan Accounting Advisory, Ltd. also withdraws its offer to you.

Best regards,
J.M. Smith
Attorney

As we gained more experience in China, we realized that for our specific situation, Jackson's value was that of a glorified translator—with the legal work provided mostly by Steven. Jackson's only previous experience with food business was not directly relevant to our baking business—registering the gelato business for the Italian contact that referred us to the law firm. In hindsight, instead of the few thousand US dollars that Jackson's services should have cost, we heard that the poor Italian entrepreneur paid him over $50,000. The process was not smooth, and caused the owner, a large Italian man, to break down crying on several occasions.

In our case, when Jackson switched our registration from a restaurant management firm to a restaurant firm, the advice essentially prevented us from franchising—our highest priority as we had emphasized when we hired him.

We were without an agent once again.

The Firm
Registration Nightmare

May to June, 2008

"Your choices," the health bureau official, whom I nicknamed the Opportunist, informed Joe and our new agent, Tian Baoyu, "are either not open or simply choose to not sell pretzels. You can sell drinks. But not pretzels. It is against the law."

After getting fired by Jackson Smith, we had to resort to using local agents again. Based on multiple recommendations and many interviews with potential agents, we chose Tian Baoyu.

Tian Baoyu was an accountant by trade and owned a small accounting firm with a few employees. In her mid-thirties, she had ventured to Beijing alone. After struggling to make ends meet to launch her own firm, she had become a tough lady. We found her a good fit to help fight our case because of her feistiness, although she was also good at negotiating her fees. She was around five feet, four inches tall, with a pleasant, pretty face and figure.

Often, accountants performed the registration work in hopes of picking up annual business to provide tax services. Tian Baoyu successfully registered one of our friend's restaurants, so she was, to our understanding, "highly referred." Supposedly, she had many contacts inside of the Health Bureau.

The first store at the Gate Mall on the west side of Beijing was fully constructed, with the equipment installed and tested. We had already invested over $100,000 USD into construction and equipment. There was one little problem: selling pretzels at that store was 'illegal,' according to the Opportunist.

The pretzel was an unknown product in China. There was no consistent translation for the word, so we coined our own Chinese name. As a result, in the eyes of the regulatory bureaus' business perspective, we had essentially created a new category. No one knew how to manage it. They did know, however, that our $100,000 undertaking was too small to be a full bakery but too complex to be merely a point of sale location, and involved too many types of raw ingredients—hot dogs, fresh lemons, and drinks—to be a single snack store. In essence, determining our category of business was subjective—left to be determined by each individual health bureau agent. And that fact, inevitability, left us vulnerable to corruption.

"Madam, may we get a copy of the health bureau code?" Joe followed up, conjuring his most polite voice. The Health Bureau in Haidian District (the west side of Beijing) was only open for initial submission two days per week, for a total of four hours each day. The facilities contained an open seating area in the front and a separate holding area for the people waiting for their booth to be opened. With numbered stalls behind thick glass partitions, this facility could have doubled as a bank. Furniture and tables were faded from extensive use. The air conditioning was technically on, but the air so weak I would have preferred a fan. Bureau employees behind the glass partitions must have enjoyed strong, cool air conditioning, as many of them were wearing long sleeves.

Standing in line was no easy task, as dozens of filthy-looking guys in unkempt clothing were angling and squeezing behind Joe and Tian Baoyu. These were low-paid runners working for equally low-paid agents. Most were barely literate, but their value lay in the fact that they had time to spare to wait in line and a talent for pushing their way to the front. As there were no numbers to show a person's place in line, we found ourselves subjects of a Darwinian experiment as to who was stronger in pushing and angling, one that truly defined the phrase "every man for himself." The scene was very primal. Look away for a second too long and there may be a new person squeezed in front. Given the strict government regulations on every aspect of life in China, visitors would be surprised by anarchy while waiting in line.

As Joe and Tian Baoyu braved the experiment, I waited for them both in the open area, holding bags of paperwork we brought in case the Opportunist requested it. The guys behind them were not pushing per se, but instead filled every available open space, and had to push to do so. The stench from a mixture of sweat and body odor permeated the air on this hot, humid summer day, but it was nothing compared to the rhythmic hot air blowing on the backs of Joe and Tian Baoyu's necks—the result of the heated exhalations of the men in line behind them. Their breath was disgusting and violating, to say the least. The odor was not the residual of a meal, but rather bacteria and grime from weeks of leaving teeth un-brushed, resembling the smell of dried vomit. Many of the aggressive line pushers had never met a toothbrush in their lives.

"The health code is very well documented, and so are the laws," the Opportunist declared with authority from behind the glass barrier in her booth, marked '#4,' assumedly to give the illusion that the building had any conceivable sense of order. "Just ask anyone and they can get you a copy." She was patting a large, textbook-sized manual that must have been the mysterious health code. Tian Baoyu had been helping people register restaurants for years, and she had never gotten copies of this mysterious document.

"Well, since we are here, may we buy a copy, madam? We are more than happy pay for it." Joe offered a big smile, doubling his efforts to be nice and gracious despite having waited in this place for hours.

"Stop wasting my time! The laws are well-documented. You did not follow the law, so I cannot approve the store. Go fix it and come back!" the Opportunist concluded impatiently, glancing anxiously at the long lines of people in front of her booth.

Joe continued to be relentlessly shoved by the crowd gathering behind him. Up until then, Tian Baoyu had been boxing out the pushers, with effort that would have made a basketball coach proud. But she was getting overpowered, and the pushing became more aggressive with each passing minute.

"But…but you advised us how to design the store the last time we were here!" Joe tried to respond more aggressively. "You put in these changes. They are your designs! I do not understand how it is possible—"

"NEXT!" the Opportunist concluded, cutting off Joe mid-sentence. "Go fix these issues and come back."

With that, our approval process was delayed another week.

There were multiple booths serving different functions for the Health Bureau. We had been here several times and had always worked with the Opportunist, so we needed to make sure that we continued with her. She had approved our designs last week. We had entered her booth that afternoon under the apparently misguided notion that we simply needed to return and retrieve her final chop, or stamp, on our store's architectural drawings.

Two to three agents were responsible for reviewing applications and visiting sites for all new restaurant applications. Their schedules were such that they spent two days per week reviewing or giving advice on applications submitted through these front windows. The rest of the time they traveled to the sites for final approval. Many businesses were trying to open before the Olympics, creating a rush of applications and site visits. We had hoped to simply get the Opportunist's final approval and then schedule a store visit later in the week.

As it was our first store, we wanted to follow every law possible and not go the "local" way (which may involve bribing or gift-giving) as our friends in the area had suggested. Yet, we were stuck in an impossible situation. We needed to abide by changing laws that, unbeknownst to us, were enforced by low-wage, corrupt government employees looking for their true payday. How could we do this without breaking laws?

This was when Mr. Pang came to the rescue.

Good Enough
for Health License

June to July 2008

Mr. Pang looked like an aspiring Hong Kong triad member. He was shorter than I, to the extent that I could use the reflection from his perfectly-shaved head as a mirror. His cheap clubbing clothing contrasted the fact that he drove a $100,000 Audi A6. The toothpick he constantly held in his mouth was one of his standout features, but not as much as his two-inch pinky nail digging in and out of his ears, not to mention his ability to flick his earwax.

Mr. Pang was a man who had true inside connections with the Haidian District Health Bureau. While others were frantically pushing their way up to the front, he sat and waited calmly and patiently on the benches. I watched him during one visit. Confidence to the point of cockiness oozed from his pose. He waited for maybe ten minutes and then received a phone call. Immediately after, he walked past the area where all the people were pushing, to the employee entrance. The door quickly opened, and he was ushered in, along with all the documents he carried. Upon exiting twenty minutes later, we watched as several people jumped out of line to ask for his help. Many shoved wads of cash at him to review their documentation and help push their applications along.

Tian Baoyu explained that Mr. Pang had reliable connections inside the bureaus. With the government's heavy crackdown on graft, bureau members were afraid to take bribes directly from people they did not know, and therefore relied on the Mr. Pangs of Beijing as intermediaries. There were only a few people like him per district, as they kept their circles small—in fact, most other firms or people who advertised their great "connections" inside the bureau were likely referring to Mr. Pang. His $100,000 car proved how profitable managing the "consulting" for just one district's Health Bureau could be.

"How come Mr. Pang could not submit this paperwork for us?" Joe asked Tian Baoyu, after the Opportunist rejected our paperwork. Before we submitted the paperwork, Tian Baoyu had Mr. Pang visit our store a few weeks earlier to give advice on how to change the designs to pass the bureau.

"I do not think that Mr. Pang actually knows the Opportunist," Tian Baoyu responded. "As I mentioned, his contacts are other people." We assumed he knew all the employees at the Health Bureau. In fact, there were only a few people there with whom he had mutually beneficial "relationships." When we initially submitted the paperwork, we were assigned to the Opportunist and not his contacts. He wanted us to continue with the Opportuntist and not switch since it will make the situation look suspicious.

Unlike the previous agents and lawyers, Tian Baoyu simply took our documentation and started to perform the next steps for us. She operated on her own and did not seek us for decisions, which turned out to be yet another mistake.

"Why the hell did we listen to his advice, then?" I asked. We changed our designs based on his recommendations, and that effort suddenly felt wasted.

"Cha bu duo," Tian Baoyu assured us. "We will pass this part, no problem."

Given the fact that our "pre-approved" plans were rejected, I started to feel doubt about Mr. Pang's and Tian Baoyu's connections.

But then, surprisingly, Mr. Pang proved his usefulness by being able to get the designs approved behind the scenes. His contacts reached out to the Opportunist and struck a deal. Not only did he return the documents with the right chops, he arranged the date of the official visit. Tian Baoyu received a list of to-dos from Mr. Pang to review with us in preparation of the visit.

"Most of these things are simple fixes," Tian Baoyu said, her voice taking on a cautionary tone. "Some caulking here and there. But there is one thing that Mr. Pang was more stringent about. You have a glass sliding door in the drawings in the back kitchen. Make sure that rails and the doors are fully installed."

This was in direct contradiction with the environmental bureau, whose employees had specifically informed our contractors that the rails and the screen door in the back kitchen must be removed, to allow for proper usage of the sprinklers.

Tian Baoyu recommended that we let the contractors take care of the issues, so we did not get involved in the process. We learned later that the contractor followed Mr. Pang's advice. They kept the rails and screen doors one day to pass the health bureau inspections, and then immediately removed everything so that they could pass the environmental bureau inspections.

We also heard later that the Opportunist wanted us to install an isolated dish washing room, though we only used take away containers. She was finally talked out of it.

"One other thing," Tian Baoyu said. "We need to prepare a gift card for the Opportunist. How much do you want it to be? Five hundred Renminbi (RMB)? One thousand RMB?"

"You mean a bribe?" I said. "We do not condone that you do anything illegal to get the license. No problems chatting with the Opportunist or taking her out for coffee, but nothing illegal."

"When I take her for the visit, I will figure out a time to slip it to her. Let's make it easy and get a Carrefour gift card," she said, ignoring my statement. Carrefour was the dominate player in Beijing, so their gift cards were well-received. "If you want, I can go pick it up for you, and give you a receipt later for your records."

Her attitude was incredible. She mentioned the gift card so casually, as if it was part of the application process.

"We hired you as the consultant for this matter. I am not sure what type of connections that you used in the past to obtained the license. Honestly, I do not want to know. However, please do not do anything illegal," I stressed.

"Well, if we do not offer any benefits to the Opportunist, I do not think that she will give final approval on this visit," she said. I resisted the urge to sigh, knowing that any delay could push the final approval until after the Olympic activities.

Despite Tian Baoyu's insistence that we enter the corrupt local system, our consciences simply would not allow us to present a bribe to the Opportunist. I knew this decision could delay us even more.

"Since we cannot afford any more delays, please ask more of your friends to see who can help reach out to the Opportunist and put in good words for us," I said, feeling resigned.

"Fine, if that is what you want. Please make sure you have all of these changes updated before the visit next week," Tian Baoyu concluded.

With that, our game plan was set in motion.

On July 31, 2008, with a simple paper in hand, Joe and I both nearly broke into tears. We had received our approved Health Bureau license! Finally, we could focus on how to operate Auntie Anne's, instead of wasting time on this administrative mess. After seven months of constant stress involving four agents, one law firm, countless visits to various bureaus, and hundreds of hours spent in meetings, we held in our hands the ultimate prize, the most difficult part of entire registration process—the health license.

A quick glance at it showed basic information for the company, the district and, most importantly, a chop from the health bureau to signify its full approval.

But what we saw next pushed us back to tears—the bad kind. Tian Baoyu had changed our category of business from an on-site bakery to a packaged goods dispensary. We were registered for the wrong business!

"What is this!" I screamed at her over the phone. "Why the hell are we registered for packaged goods? What does that even mean?"

"Calm down," Tian Baoyu said. "Calm down. Cha bu duo. Do not worry. No one will ever check. You wanted to get your health license before the Olympics, right? And you said to do whatever necessary to get it done, right? Well, this was the only way."

"What is the use of a license if it's registered for the wrong business?!" I continued to scream into the phone. "Explain to me what category of business you registered for our company!"

"Calm down. I will explain," she said patiently. "Packaged food simply means that you will make the food elsewhere and deliver it to the on-site location to be sold. Do not worry. A friend of mine found another friend who owns a food manufacturing plant, so we got him to chop the required documents, so you are totally fine for this category. No one will check if you are baking on-site or off-site. It is a mere technicality."

"How can it be that we cannot get the license for the onsite bakery? There is a bakery directly downstairs from us in the mall, with the same size and footprint. How did they get it?" I asked.

Tian Baoyu explained that in the time leading up to the Olympics, registration was becoming much more stringent. Difficulty of registration evolved based on who was in power.

"So, you are saying that if we did not use the packaged goods category, we cannot open in time for the Olympics?" I said.

"Yes. It is your business, so if you want me to try to change the registration, I will," she offered. "But I am telling you that it will not work. The decision is yours."

Joe and I discussed the situation and realized that we were backed into a corner. There was no simple way to look at our circumstances. If we judged the rules as only black and white, we would not survive. Most of China operated in the gray, which was unfamiliar to us. We called Tian Baoyu back a little later.

"Since you have already processed our paperwork in the packaged goods category without our consent, you give us no other options," I said. "Please continue with the next step of registration. We will update the category after we open."

Food and beverage businesses typically opened as soon as they received their health bureau license. Of all of the licenses required, not having a health license carried the most penalties. Property management turned a blind eye by allowing stores to open as long as they had their health license. Some will even go further and inform all stores without business licenses to close temporarily during official bureau visits.

To obtain a business license in the food and beverage sector in Beijing, we needed to have our health, environmental, and fire safety bureau licenses in hand, and then register at the tax bureau. These processes combined could take anywhere from four to six months. Adding stress to this procedure was the reality that, upon signing a lease to a new location, most landlords would give a very limited amount of time for construction and definitely would not allow a new tenant to be closed for six months during registration.

With our decision to move forward with the incorrect category of business, we were able to get our health bureau license in time to open for the Beijing Olympics.

Please Start Over

July to August 2008

I felt cramped in Director Shen's small office. The room was sterile, with hospital-like fluorescent lighting, a desk void of anything personal, and faded paint on the walls. The image of an interrogation room crossed my mind, which proved fitting; we felt trapped in more ways than one.

Our celebration of obtaining the health bureau license was a bit premature. After the joyous day when we received it, Tian Baoyu took the health license to the State Administration of Industry and Commerce (SAIC) to get our business license. The process, we had heard, was an easy, routine procedure that took no more than one week to complete.

Normally.

SAIC notified Tian Baoyu that the wording on the actual health bureau license did not match what we originally put on the SAIC application. The issue was a common occurrence that we had seen multiple times, since applicants often did not know what the health bureau would approve. The approval for a store to sell Chinese food, for instance, could fall under several categories, with the final decision ultimately made, once again, by the individual health bureau agent.

The irony of the situation was that we had proof from SAIC that one of their employees instructed us to get the health license first before worrying about any changes to the category of business for SAIC's purposes.

Regardless, the notice required us to start over with the health bureau application; this time, our certificate had to match the business we originally applied for. And we were back to square one.

Of course, this decision was unacceptable to us. We requested a meeting with a "decision maker" at the SAIC and were referred to Director Shen.

A little while later, Tian Baoyu, Joe, and I sat nervously as Director Shen flipped through our papers.

"So, what is the issue here?" he demanded.

"Well, our application for the business license was declined," Tian Baoyu summarized, her attitude direct, perhaps aggressively so. "The reason stated was that the category of business listed when we first formed the name here in this department was different from the category written on our license from the health bureau. The decision to—"

"Why is this an issue?" Director Shen interrupted as he continued to scan the papers in our file. "You said yourself that the category you first listed is written differently on the license. That is a legitimate reason for the rejection."

"Here is a printout from your department website of details from another company that received their business license recently," Tian Baoyu said as she handed a sheet of paper to Director Shen.

Joe and I glanced uneasily at each other as her aggressiveness turned into defiance. This seemed a dangerous attitude to take with a government employee.

"As you can see, the category of this business is different between what was listed in the health bureau and the SAIC," she continued. "This company was able to get their business license. We should be as well."

"Let me see that," Director Shen said. He looked at the paper for a few seconds, and then started to nod his head. "You are correct. They were able to get their license despite the different categories of business listed. Well, someone made a mistake there, which is unfortunate. I apologize, but that will not help your case. Just because someone from this department made a mistake doesn't mean that we can make it again knowingly, is that not correct?"

"Director Shen," Joe jumped in before Tian Baoyu answered, as he realized that Tian Baoyu had entered into an unwinnable argument. "My name is Mr. Sze, and I am the legal representative for this company. Mr. Lin and I are from the US, so we are new to the process of opening up a business here. I see the issue that you are referring to, and we wanted to ask for your help. We have been trying to open our business—and it has not been easy.

"After we found out about the change of categories from the health bureau, we came back to this department to see if we needed to submit additional paperwork to change the category of business formally. Here is a document that we received from one of the employees here, stating that we could bring the completed health bureau license back and make the change together." Joe tossed through the folder that Tian Baoyu brought and found the document to hand to Director Shen.

"Interesting." Again, Director Shen looked at the document closely. "This is not standard procedure. It looks like our employee made another mistake again. The front desk employees do not have the authorities to bypass the process. You needed to get the formal change of categories of business before getting your health bureau license. I apologize again, but I cannot approve your request. I know that we have made a few mistakes on your case here."

Only a few mistakes, I thought.

"Why don't you do this?" Director Shen offered. "Take your health bureau license back and get them to change the category to what you have listed here at this bureau. It is a simple change, from packaged food to on-site bakery. Just a few words. They can do it for you quickly and easily. No problem."

"With all due respect, sir, it has not been an easy process," Joe explained. "Far from it. The health bureau took several months longer than expected, and I know that the agent there will not make these changes for us." Joe's tone was becoming increasingly agitated and desperate.

"Please, what you are asking for us to do is to start over from the beginning," he said. "Other firms faced the same issue and were able to get over it. On top of that, we even came to ask for instructions before making any changes at the health bureau."

"I am truly sorry for the wrong instructions given by our staff. There is simply nothing I can do. I cannot approve your request," Director Shen concluded as he started to stand up. "Do not worry. I know the people at the health bureau. This change is easy for them and they will make it for you, if you explain the situation for them. It will just take a few days there to update. Then bring the updated health bureau license back and we will process it quickly."

With this, Director Shen walked us to his door. "It will be a simple change. I am sure of it. See you soon, okay?"

With that, he held the door open until we walked out. The door shut behind us.

Starting over was not an option, as we could not repeat the process at the health bureau again. The only thing we could do, we realized, was figure out how to penetrate the SAIC.

Tian Baoyu knew that we would not be starting over, either, not after all that we had been through together. We all combed our networks to find anyone with a link to the SAIC; no relationship was too small or insignificant. In the end, Tian Baoyu found another agent who claimed he could get someone to change our category of business in the system. Then, we could reapply and the paperwork would (hopefully) go through without notice to Director Shen or any other supervisor who might be familiar with our case. The plan would be risky for the person updating our paperwork, she said—"risky" being a code word for "expensive."

Expensive it was. But after eight months of grueling work, five agents, and one law firm, we did, at long last, obtain our business license. Our biggest headache disappeared instantly when we found the right guanxi.

In hindsight, if I had known then what I know now, I would have camped out in front of the health bureau or the business bureau to chat with the numerous "agents" soliciting work. Sounds almost too simple, but without pre-existing contacts, it was the quickest way to meet people who would have connections inside the bureaus. These "agents" in front of the bureaus are salespeople for those who have connections inside the bureaus. Many of the "agents" may claim more connections than they actually have, so one needs to be careful when interviewing and determining what type of contacts each "agent" has. What I have learned is that the "agents" are usually from the same region in China as the contacts that they have inside the bureaus, which makes trust and pre-existing relationships the key connection. The "agents" can work with their connections in the bureaus to give advice on how to fill out the paperwork properly and facilitate the submission process. For a fee, of course.

Drip 3

Almost Open

Learning to be an Entrepreneur

My first few months into entrepreneurship sucked. All the stories about successful entrepreneurs usually focus on the glory of the great companies they built, but glanced over the extreme pains they suffered to get there. No one told me about the details of these initial pains. The first casualty was that my relationships with both new acquaintances and close friends changed for the worse.

Money. I hate to mention it, but money caused some major headaches between Karen and I. Joe and I had allotted modest salaries for ourselves, but we ended up not taking most of that money because we wanted the business to show profit before we took home anything. In effect, we chose to live on our savings.

Karen was a consultant at McKinsey and Company, and both of us were used to the luxury of generous expense accounts. That life ended for me. I used to peruse the menu for items that I wanted to eat, but now I filtered by prices only. Selecting what I wanted became second priority; filling my stomach was first. I had grown up believing that the man was supposed to be the breadwinner of the household, and it was difficult to impose the sacrifices of an entrepreneur on Karen. Whenever she wanted to go shopping or enjoy an upscale restaurant, I felt uneasy about the expense. My hesitation and reluctance to do anything "expensive" became a sore subject, as everything we did before was considered "expensive."

Going out with friends for a night of drinking used to be nothing but joyous. Now, going out had many limitations. If someone picked too high end of a place, I would make up random excuses and not go. The worst feeling was when I made conscious decisions not to order expensive things but then someone suggests splitting the bill evenly. I felt uneasy bringing up the subject of money with friends, so the whole experience of going out with friends was not as enjoyable as before.

Besides money, I felt myself becoming more sensitive to criticisms. When did everyone become an expert on opening pretzel stores? Off the cuff criticisms from friends on areas where I thought we excelled hurt deeply. One negative comment could ruin my day. Thinking back to all the times I made random suggestions to other entrepreneurs on things that they should do better, I felt like an ass for doing so. After a while, instead of becoming defensive, I learned to accept it as good willed suggestions and took it at face value.

When we first arrived, we met with as many people in the restaurant industry as we could. One observation I made about human behavior during this time was that the successful entrepreneurs truly wanted to help, and the people who had failed seemed to be cheering for us to fail.

Perhaps the most useful contact that we had were the owners of one of the most successful chains of Chinese food restaurants in China (think about the significance of that). The couple who ran the chain was referred through one of Joe's friends. Without even knowing us well at the time, they graciously allowed us to leverage their hard earned government guanxi to navigate the registration processes for future stores.

On the other hand, a similar referral to an owner of a struggling small restaurant that eventually closed led to dinners and drinks on multiple occasions where that person quizzed us on all aspects of our business. The person kept mentioning how difficult the market was and what type of contacts he had. Yet, his offers to help us never materialized. He did, however, kept checking in on us to see how we were doing. My gut told me he felt happy when I told him bad news about our business and he got jealous or upset when I told him good news.

The best thing about this trying period of adjusting to being an entrepreneur was that I became more resourceful in everything I did. Every resource we had was limited, so we had to stretch it out as much as possible. The example that makes me proudest was the establishment of the internship program.

It started as a joke. Kramerica Industries was a fake firm started by Kramer on the TV show *Seinfeld* and run by an intern from NYU named Darren. Friends and I joked often that we should hire interns to explore our entrepreneurial ideas.

The joke surfaced again over drinks with friends in early 2008, before Joe and I had hired any employees for our franchise. Only now, we were not laughing. We were in desperate need of someone who could read and write Chinese to help us with writing our initial job descriptions and hiring. And just like that, Darren the intern became an action plan.

Our timing was perfect, as the unemployment rate for new graduates in China was very high in early 2008. Students were applying for all sorts of opportunities, trying to improve their chances of having a job when they graduated. We designed internships programs that sounded exclusive and made sure that students would have tangible results to show for.

Students would never have to do menial tasks like making copies or getting coffee. There was a fruit juice company in Beijing that ended up hiring unpaid interns from the University of North Carolina at Chapel Hill. Eager, hungry, and ambitious, these interns showed up ready to learn about doing big business in China, only to get their hunger literally satisfied. Their first assignment? Cut fruit. "Intern! Make sure that the orange peel gets removed completely, or else it will make the juice bitter." "Intern! Pop quiz! What types of knives are best suited to cut carrots, and what kinds should be used to cut pineapples?" Welcome to China. Eight hours per day, they cut away.

Our internships would be different. We posted the opportunity with some top universities in Beijing and received an overwhelming number of requests. The applicants completed a detailed application in English and underwent three rounds of interviews. In the end, we hired ten interns from various backgrounds such as law, business and English.

These interns helped us set up and implement our initial back office, from hiring our first set of managers and employees to brainstorming for marketing campaigns. The quality was good, though we had to overcome many cultural differences to reach the final results.

One interesting revelation we had in our experience with interns was that the teaching style in local Chinese school systems focused on memorization over critical thinking. Students were taught to memorize and follow directions.

My only exposure to the Chinese education system was when I took the exam for my Chinese driver's license. Out of the 1,300 or so practice questions, several questions provided officially incorrect answers, so it was up to the test taker to memorize the answers as stated in the practice exams. The difficult part was when a question had the correct answer in the true and false section of the test, but not in the multiple-choice section.

This difference in thinking often led to cultural differences in the workplace. A friend of ours, who was a lawyer with a US law firm in

Beijing, was working with a graphic design firm on some marketing materials for his firm's clients. The marketing firm operated in English but had mostly local Chinese employees, and there were constant misunderstandings. In one instance, a set of designs created by the graphic design firm diverged drastically from his expectations. He was so upset that he crossed out the designs and scribbled "WTF" ("What the fuck?") in bright red marker over it, and promptly faxed it back to show his displeasure.

The marketing firm did not respond for several days as they worked to redesign the logo and marketing push. Hours of creative effort were poured into the project. The result was a new set of logos featuring none other than the new name of the marketing campaign: WTF.

The cultural gaps resulted in constant miscommunication. I would ask someone to do task A, but task D would get completed. Closing the cultural gap was similar to learning a new language. Often, I had to explain something five or six times in different words to ensure that the right message was understood. Once I learned how to explain that one thing well, I would apply the same tactic to a similar category to see if it worked. The process was exhausting yet necessary. Time and patience were the two biggest factors to not go crazy.

My entire world was turned upside down in the first few months as an entrepreneur, from my relationships with others to my approach to everything I did. Although these experiences were challenging already, I could not fathom what awaited us next.

The Blinding Experience

"Wen-Szu, this is Carlie." Her voice was rapid and frantic. "Something has happened to Joe! It's his eyes. He cannot see. It's the same thing that happened to Katrina and Fiona earlier today." Over the phone, her voice trailed off; she sounded on the verge of tears. "I do not know what to do... C-c-can—can you come up?"

Carlie was calling from their condo apartment upstairs from mine. She was taking care of Joe and two of our investors, Fiona and Katrina. The two women had been complaining about irritation in their eyes on the way home from an all-day training at the store. Joe experienced similar pains shortly after he returned home. By this point, we had finished construction on the first store, had hired our first set of employees, and had started in-store training to teach the employees how to make a pretzel.

Fiona and Katrina are sisters in their 30s and late 20s, respectively, and of Chinese descent though born and raised in Idaho. Their parents own and operate a Chinese restaurant in their hometown, so they grew up in the kitchen. While Katrina stayed in Idaho to help out with the family business, Fiona attended the Culinary Institute of America and is now a pastry chef in LA. Their family invested in Auntie Anne's China, and the women arrived in Beijing the week before to assist with the initial employee training.

I quickly relayed the conversation to my wife, Karen. Karen had not yet moved to Beijing in mid-2008, and was visiting for the weekend. She suggested that I find out if our other employees were experiencing the same symptoms before going up to Joe's place. I called the store manager Sun Wang, who was in charge of managing the employees' schedules that day. Sun Wang is from Dongbei (Northeast) region of China, which has a reputation of being a home for tough guys who like to fight. Verbal arguments often are settled through fist fights, according to the region's reputation. Coincidentally, the few Dongbei guys that we had on staff were all fairly big, thick-boned, and mean-looking, though Sun Wang's thin-rimmed, dirty silver glasses gave his dark, leathery face, a soft appeal despite the deep acne scars from his youth.

Given that reputation, I was surprised when I heard Sun Wang's voice over the phone. Our tough Dongbei manager was crying. Between sniffles, Sun Wang sobbed that he could not see. He shared an apartment with a few other employees, and I knew that he kept in close contact with the rest. He mentioned that he was not the only one either; all of the employees were essentially blinded.

I quickly asked Sun Wang what he thought the reason could be. He had no clue, but randomly threw out that we had received some new cleaning solutions in unmarked bottles.

I began to panic. Trying to gain some type of control back, I turned my panic into anger. I wanted some answers for Carlie before I went upstairs, and so far I had nothing. I made one last phone call.

The cleaning products supplier was not expecting the rage and barrage of accusations about to come. With a loud, forceful voice foreign to me, I screamed something to the effect of "You son of a bitch! What the hell did you sell me?!" into the receiver. "Did you know that your crappy, poisonous products blinded half my employees?! We have over 20 people right now that cannot see!"

"Uhhh...what...uhhh...what are you talking about?" the supplier fumbled. "I only brought over some basic disinfectant and some—"

"Some poisonous crap!" I was gaining strength from yelling at him. I realized that there was no way this guy would admit to anything, assuming he had done anything wrong in the first place.

"Your piece of crap supplies blinded all of our people. Go figure out what did it, or else I am going to report you!" With that, I hung up on him. In China, a person or a business reported to the government bureaus could result in many investigations into his or her business and accounts, something no businessperson want to experience. As unreal as it sounds, I felt some control return to me.

Upstairs, meanwhile, Carlie did not rest after our conversation. Instead, she grabbed for her mobile phone and searched for Joyce's number. Joyce worked in hospital management in Beijing and would know what to do.

"Joyce! Carlie here. I need your help." Carlie spoke as calmly as she could when her friend answered. Before Joyce could say a word, she poured the whole story out.

"Whoa, slow down, slow down," Joyce said. "Let's take it back one step. You are saying that Joe and your friends are in a lot of pain. And they cannot see anymore?"

"Yes, exactly. We trained new employees in the store all day, but they only felt the pain on the way home," Carlie said.

"Wait, wait...when you said 'we,' were you there as well?"

"Yes." Carlie paused to understand the significance of Joyce's question. "Yes, I was, but there is nothing wrong with my eyes. I am perfectly fine."

"I am out at dinner with a local doctor friend of mine. We are not too far from you." Joyce said. "Do you want to go to the hospital directly now, or do you want us to come over?"

Carlie did not hesitate. "Well, I would not even know how to get to a hospital or which one to go to. Wen-Szu is coming over. Can you come over as well?"

"Sure, we'll leave right away. See you in twenty."

Karen and I hurried upstairs to Joe's apartment around 10 p.m. The living room was abnormally silent and dark when we entered. Creepy shadows flickered across the room in the dusty yellow light from the small lamp in the corner. Faint groans from several people in pain echoed softly. Fiona and Katrina were curled up in a ball on the L-shaped couch with their arms hugging their shins. Katrina was sniffling a little, as if she had been crying for a while. Joe's two arms stretched straight in front of him as he floated towards me from the darkness, reminding me of a zombie from *Return of the Living Dead*.

As we waited for Joyce and her doctor friend, we all talked, wracking our brains to see if we could figure out what could have caused the blindness. Fiona, Katrina, and Joe all said that their eyes felt like they were being rubbed with sandpaper and stuck with pins.

"Damn it! What the hell happened?" Joe yelled suddenly. Tears started to stream down the side of his face as he swung his arms out in the air as if trying to punch an invisible monster. "I hate this place!"

When he had calmed down, I spoke. "Before I came up, I called Sun Wang and he told me that all of our employees are experiencing the same pain. He only communicated with the store level employees, so I am not sure about the other managers. What did you do today at the store?"

"We clarified butter all day," Joe said. "Besides that, the contractors were there all day making small repairs here and there. The employees were cleaning all morning."

"Not sure if it helps, but I was a little burned here," Carlie pointed to the area above her shirt. "I do not know what it's from, but the skin is a bit darker."

We were interrupted by a knock on the door. Carlie jumped up from the couch and ran to answer, letting in Joyce and her doctor friend.

Joyce's friend did a quick examination of Joe's eyes and said we should go to the emergency room immediately.

"What have you told the employees so far?" Joyce asked me as Carlie and Karen started to prep Joe, Fiona, and Katrina to go to the hospital.

"Nothing yet. I just called one manager to ask about his situation, and he told me about the other employees," I explained.

"Good, you need to control the information. Be fact-driven and do not try to elaborate too much," Joyce warned. "In fact, you may not want to call them at all, but if you do, let them know that we are researching the situation. If they feel the need, please let them go to the hospital as soon as possible."

I felt a stab of guilt. I wanted to call the employees and order them to the hospital, but I did not want to start a panic. Instead I called the managers and instructed them to share the instructions Joyce had given.

My three blinded colleagues stood up, latching on to the people assisting them. Imagine seeing three people with their eyes swollen shut, faces flushed from pain with tears still rolling down their cheeks, and arms outstretched in front of them stumbling out onto a dark street at night. The scene looked like a Halloween prank gone horribly wrong.

✼ ✼ ✼

Joyce's doctor friend suggested a local hospital not too far away with an emergency wing that could handle eye injuries. He called to inform them that some emergency cases were coming in.

As we walked Joe, Fiona, and Katrina into the emergency room, we pulled three numbers from a ticket machine and sat on the worn-out benches to wait. Slow healthcare is one of the downsides of having 1.2 billion people, and Beijing is a good place to witness it. There would be hundreds of people waiting in line to grab a number early in the morning. With the number in hand, they usually had to wait all day before they could see the doctor for a few minutes. If the number was called and the patient was not there, the number was forfeited and they would need to get another one. There were even entrepreneurs who line up early to grab a number so they could sell it to people who show up late. Every bench seat, however loose from wear and tear, is full all day with people sleeping while they wait. There were so many people waiting in the corridors that it feels more like being at a rock concert. One doctor might see dozens of patients in the span of a single hour. Not surprisingly, these overworked doctors are prone to mistakes and bad attitudes. Facilities were worn from overuse, and the equipment is antique. There was not a single comforting thought or a sight for someone who was used to Western facilities and medicine.

But that night we were in luck, as the emergency room did not have a long line. As we waited, one of our managers, Zhu Boxing, called us and said that he was also going to the hospital, so we coordinated for him to join us.

After only fifteen minutes or so of waiting, the doctor was able to see Joe.

The doctor looked in Joe's eyes with a retinoscope and immediately recognized that they had been burned with something. Given what we knew, we asked him if it could be a chemical burn. He said yes.

He dripped some prescription eye drops into Joe's eyes. As the drops landed, a big smile suddenly formed on Joe's face, wiping away the look of agony he had worn all night.

"That is freakin' awesome!" he cried. "What the hell was that? The pain is gone!"

The doctor looked relieved, but quickly shuffled Joe out to treat Fiona and Katrina.

The doctor gave his patients some bottles of antibiotic eye drops, but cautioned them to use them sparingly so as not to lessen the relieving effects. The pain, he said, would come back as badly for a few days, and the burn would take a few weeks to fully heal.

Our China hospital experience turned out to be quite good and efficient, to my pleasant surprise. Complete relief was an understatement, as we now knew everyone would be all right. To top it off, the overall cost for the exam and eye drops was only a few hundred RMB for everyone—under $50 US dollars.

As we prepared to leave, Zhu Boxing's girlfriend called to inform us that they had arrived, but in a different part of the hospital. Though Joe still looked like a mess and was starting to be in pain again, he said that he wanted to go see Zhu Boxing to show support. After all Joe had gone through that day, it was a courageous, well-intentioned effort on his part. Carlie, Karen, and I helped guide him as Joyce took Katrina and Fiona back to Joe's apartment.

Zhu Boxing was our first hire for Auntie Anne's. He had a very cheerful, open attitude, and the ability to befriend most people. I have seen him make strangers laugh with a simple question, get silent people to talk to him by offering a cigarette, and earn the trust of employees through smooth speeches. If he lived in the US, he would make a killing as a car salesman or even as a smooth-talking consultant. Unfortunately, he proved to be very conniving and always tried to find unethical methods to take short cuts or profit personally. His effectiveness at persuasion was great if he was on your side, but he could be deadly if crossed.

Zhu Boxing played an important role in our experience with Auntie Anne's, both good and bad, so it was fitting that he was the first employee we met up with at the start of the blinding experience. When I saw him, his face was also flush from the pain and the tears. His skin also looked darker than before, which made the newly formed wrinkles, caused by squinting, besides his eyes visible. Joe and Zhu Boxing tried to joke about the event, but all they could afford was a forced chuckle. Surprisingly, Joe reached out to give him a hug. Both Joe and Zhu Boxing could hardly see, had tears rolling down the side of their faces, and moved clumsily towards each other. It felt like a reunion of two combat veterans who had suffered major injuries together. In a strange way, it was touching to see.

On the way home, we planned what we needed to do the next day to discover the root causes of the blinding. It was a weekend, so we were not conducting full training. Two employees would be there to watch over the store. At that point, we had only a handful of random clues but no exact understanding of what had happened.

Our ideas were nothing close to the truth.

The Hidden Light

Truth be told, I went to bed fearing not the cause of the blindness, but the onslaught of potential lawsuits. This fear of legal repercussions motivated me to press hard to uncover the root cause of the whole fiasco. Despite Joe's continued pain, I know that he agreed.

Joe, Fiona, Katrina, and close to twenty employees were all blinded after a normal day of training. How? I asked myself as Karen and I returned from the hospital. The last thing I wanted to do was dwell on this issue. Bags had started forming under my eyes from fatigue; yet sleep would not come. My stomach churned and my mind would not shut off.

"Well, let's go over what they were doing all day. They were preparing butter and they cleaned the store. Did they do anything else?" Karen said. Though Karen was a management consultant at one of the top strategy consulting firms in the world, I hardly saw the analytical side of her at home. Like many people of Filipino heritage, she was usually carefree and easy-going.

"As far as I know, that was all they did all day," I said. "But a bunch of other things happened besides the blinding part."

"We know that they used the cleaning solution from the new supplier today. What exactly is this 84? What does it do and why did it come in unmarked bottles?" Karen asked.

One thing we had learned was many industrial solutions used at restaurants in China came from local suppliers who offered low prices. However, the downside was that they use recycled bottles which were often unmarked. Suppliers buy the solution in large quantities and then manually divide it up into smaller bottles to capitalize on the quantity discount. Most likely, they also added some sort of "fillers" to make the solution more diluted to lower their cost. For example, hand soaps in restaurants in low priced restaurants in China are occasionally diluted with water to save the owners money.

"I think one other cleaning solution was delivered today, but could not remember which one. Let me call Ankang to see what 84 is."

Ankang's family had operated Chinese restaurants for nearly a decade in Singapore and for over five years in Beijing. He was the contact who referred us to this supplier. Also, he had been a reliable advisor for our restaurant and supplier-related questions. I had texted him earlier to inform him of the blinding incident and my suspicions that it could be related to his supplier.

The phone only rang twice before Ankang picked up. Before I could even say hello, he blurted "Hi Wen-Szu? How's Joe? What happened?"

"Hi Ankang, thanks for the concern. Do not have much time to explain now, but can I ask you a few questions?" I asked.

"Sure, anything. Hey, by the way, I am sorry for the supplier. We have never had an issue with him before." Ankang had genuine guilt in his voice.

"It's okay. It's not your fault. What is this 84 solution used for?" I asked.

"It is a disinfectant. It can be quite potent, depending on how it is used. We use it to disinfect the counters and floors, and we also use it to clean the wok at the end of the night. We put 84 and boiling water into the wok so that we can scrub the grease out of it."

"Is it so potent that it can cause burns to the eye or skin?"

"Well, none of our employees ever touch it directly with their hands since it can be pretty strong. When they have to touch it, they usually wear rubber gloves, but I...I am not sure if it can cause burns like that," Ankang hesitated on the phone as he thought. "If the solution was mixed with other chemicals, anything is possible. Otherwise, it probably can be, but we need to see the specific batch to see how potent it is."

I thanked Ankang for his time and recounted his thoughts to Karen.

"Besides the 84, what other clues do we have? One very important clue is that Carlie was there all day, but she was okay," Karen said. "Wait. Is she not the only person who was okay from the entire group?"

"You're right! That is pretty weird that she was not affected at all," I said.

"Was she involved in all of the training and cleaning?"

"Actually, I do not know 100 percent, but I doubt if she was cleaning. I think only the employees were cleaning. But I could see her help Fiona and Katrina train others on clarifying butter."

As I thought about the process of clarifying butter, it reminded me of something that became instantly disturbing. Typical butter at the grocery store has two parts, milk and pure clarified butter. For Auntie Anne's, we only used the pure clarified butter, so we had to remove the milk. This process entailed melting blocks of butter in the microwave so the two parts would separate, with the lighter clarified butter on top and denser milk below. We then poured the top layer of piping-hot clarified butter into disposable plastic cartons and discarded the milky portions.

Guess who bought the plastic cartons they used that day? Me. When I was shopping that week for the plastic cartons, I could have bought a more expensive, thicker plastic carton, but I opted for the cheaper version. Saving on costs seemed like a good idea at the time.

Oh crap, I thought. *Perhaps the cheap plastic melted and released toxic fumes. If this was the cause, then the blinding would be my fault. Should I admit this to Karen?*

"How can clarifying the butter burn the eyes, though? It does not make sense," Karen said. "Also, did you mention that Joe and Zhu Boxing had burns on the backs of their necks? Carlie had a burn on the top of her blouse, right? What can cause that?"

"I have no clue," I said, choosing not to discuss my concerns about the plastic cartons. I was not sure why I made the mental decision to hide something so small, but by this point in the night, I was not thinking straight.

Meanwhile, my imagination helped me along by going into overdrive. I thought about Joe pouring hot butter into the plastic carton while Sun Wang, Zhu Boxing, Katrina, Fiona, and the rest of the employees huddled in to get a better view. As he was pouring, little did they know that the plastic was melting. The carton released an invisible poisonous gas into the air and seeped into everyone's exposed skin. Since everyone was leaning in, they were getting the full effects of the invisible poison. Their eyes, their skin, and maybe even their shirts were getting burned. Guilt swept over me as I played this scene in my mind over and over.

The saint sitting on my right shoulder wanted to confess right then and there, and tell everyone that it was my fault. The devil gripping my left should kept saying, "Cover your ass. Do not admit to anything. Deny everything." At two in the morning, there was no clear winner.

"That is basically all of the information that we have," Karen concluded. "We need to see what this 84 solution is tomorrow and then go to the site to see if there could be other causes that no one saw today."

I agreed with her approach. There was nothing else to do except try to catch a few hours of sleep.

✵ ✵ ✵

At 9:30 a.m., Karen and I arrived at the mall, where we met up with the two employees who were watching the store that day. The mall did not open for another half hour, but because our employees were new and did not have mall IDs, none of us could enter. In China, all food industry-related employees needed to obtain full medical checkups at designated hospitals before they were allowed to receive mall employee IDs.

Both of these employees had been at the training as well, and their skin looked a bit darker today. They explained that they had been in pain and unable to see for most of the night. They still experienced sensations of throbbing needles in their eyes. I applauded the bravery and work ethic it took to show up early that morning.

We decided that the entire back area where they had been clarifying the butter should be quarantined off. The employees sat upfront by the register while we went to Carrefour next door to purchase our supplies. We bought a fan to blow out any potentially poisonous airborne items, bright yellow rubber dishwashing gloves for inspecting everything in the back, and large, goofy, white-rimmed face masks to protect our eyes. It was surreal.

Dressed in our silly homemade hazmat suits, we ventured into the back of the kitchen as if we were walking into a nuclear war zone. We walked one small, careful step at a time, lifting each knee with each step, as if there were invisible obstacles to dodge. After about five steps, we realized that we were moving too slowly and behaving stupidly, so we resumed our normal pace.

We set up the fan to blow air out the back door, and then we ventured slowly into the back kitchen. The room was about 20 square meters and shaped like a triangle. Situated against the walls in order were one double door stainless steel refrigerator, three sinks, two wide steel shelves for storing raw ingredients, a self-standing safe with equipment for the video cameras situated on top, one small desk for paperwork, and one waist-high freezer with a microwave on top. This had a long, blue light bulb on top that resembled a mosquito light, and was turned off. There was a small one square meter closet where we put our buckets and other cleaning supplies. The employees had been working on top of the freezer to clarify the butter and the microwave was situated there for convenience.

To be honest, we were a bit nervous, so we treated everything like it could kill us. I touched everything thinking, "Maybe it is this... no... this, or this."

As for the 84, I found the unmarked jugs of the solution and I poured some into a bowl. It was a clear solution with a hint of bluish green—just like a normal cleaning solution. I moved in closer and lifted up the edge of my mask so that I could waft some of the smell to my nose. The liquid smelled like pool water; diluted chlorine, nothing more. I looked around for other solutions and chemicals that someone could have mixed with it to create a deadly compound, but did not find anything of use. And with that, hypothesis #1 was out the door.

Nervously, I moved on to hypothesis #2: the plastic containers. I asked the two employees how they clarified the butter the previous day. They mentioned that they only poured the butter into the plastic containers after the butter was completely cooled down, which meant that the plastic could not have melted. I inspected the containers closely to see if they had any odd smells. Finding none, I gave one to Karen and told her my hypothesis. She looked the container over and dismissed it, concluding that it was good quality plastic.

Thank god I had not caused this mess directly. Only now, I was out of ideas about what had happened.

Three hours into the investigation, Karen and I took a break to go to lunch. Joe called to tell us what he learned after speaking with our general contractor, Contractor Li. Apparently, Contractor Li's employee Tao had also had eye issues as well as burns on the top of his bald head after being in the store for most of the day to fix up a few things. This was interesting, because Tao had been nowhere near the employees when they were clarifying butter. Karen and I chatted through this new piece of information and realized that the root cause must have come from something situated high up, as there were burns to people's head, parts of their necks, and chest areas.

I recalled that Contractor Li had described Tao's injuries as "sunburns." The only item that came up as a possible culprit was the blue light above the freezer. Karen immediately pulled out her blackberry and started to look up terms such as "black light" and "kitchen blue light." She discovered that UV lights were often used in kitchens to kill germs.

As these lights radiate UV rays, however, they should only be used during off hours when no one was around. Karen continued searching and read about the effects of UV rays on eyes and humans. The search results used some of the same terminology that our employees and Joe used, right down to severe burns and feelings of "sand paper rubbing against the eye," "throbbing pain," and the feeling of "pins in the eye." The light sounded more and more like the source of the problem.

Other information she found was scary. Supposedly, direct exposure to UV rays for even ten seconds could cause major burns to the pupil. The damage would depend on the strength of the UV light itself, but no websites we found mentioned effects of prolonged exposure to direct UV light from these bulbs. Our employees were under the light for four-plus hours!

I called Joe to ask if he remembered seeing the lights on.

"I think I know what it is! It's the UV lights above the freezer!" he exclaimed as soon as he picked up. I have been talking to Contractor Li for the past hour and we realized that it had to be the lights."

"Funny, I was calling to mention the UV light," I responded, feeling relieved that we had a logical explanation. "Did you see it turned on yesterday, though?"

"Yes, it was definitely on. During training, I stared into it for a while because I thought it was pretty. But I never thought to ask why it was on or what it was used for," Joe responded sheepishly.

"Who the hell turned on those lights?" I asked. "And why do we need those lights anyhow? No one ordered those. I did not."

"Tao turned it on. He did not know what it was, either, only that Contractor Li asked him to install it. Tao was testing the electrical connections in the morning and turned on everything. He forgot to turn it off. Contractor Li explained to me that the health bureau requires that all back kitchens have a UV light. No one ever uses it, but we need it for the health license. He bought it and installed it though it was not on the equipment list."

The UV lights explained everything except why Carlie's eyes had not been affected. After we called her, though, we learned that she wore contact lens with high UV protection. Another mystery solved.

Based on the information we found, there was no direct cure for the exposure to UV rays. The only thing was to let the eyes heal naturally, which was a painful process. We then informed our employees about the light and what to expect about the healing process.

Zhu Boxing and Sun Wang were familiar with this light when we told them about it, and suddenly realized in hindsight that it could have been on. They were feeling a bit guilty since they saw it was turned on, knew what it could do, and yet did not do anything to turn it off. Regardless, we wanted to manage the information given to the employees so that it was based on fact and gave them room to seek medical help if they felt the need to. We also did not want to give ammunition for the employees to sue us.

Though we were scared of the repercussions, discussing the root cause with the employees made the overall issue seem small and trivial. They experienced a sun burn, and it would fade in a few days. The UV bulb was not too strong, so thankfully there was no long term damage for anyone.

In the US, this case would have unfolded very differently. Employees would have gathered evidence from doctors, contractors, and other employees, and would have filed a lawsuit. There was good chance that we would have settled and lost a big chunk of our investment dollars.

Shockingly, after one or two days as the pain and effects disappeared, this entire issue dissipated, and no employees ever brought it up again to this day. Looking back, we thought that they did not sue us for several reasons—mainly because most of the employees did not go to the doctors and so had no physical evidence, and because the symptoms went away in a few days.

After Fiona and Katrina returned to the US, they never offered to help us again with training. They must have been quite traumatized. In fact, Katrina stopped all communications with us and did not even respond to emails where we asked basic questions. Given that we nearly blinded our own investors, I guess this was not surprising.

As for the supplier, I called and apologized for wrongly accusing him. Although I thought he would be pissed at me, he was relieved that nothing serious had happened. Still, we stopped buying from him and started to buy only branded solutions to be safe.

Auntie Anne's Opens in China

The excitement for the upcoming Olympics started to grow exponentially all over Beijing as we made our final preparations for Auntie Anne's China opening. Small but noticeable things started happening all over the city. First, it became cleaner by the day. Fines were given out for spitting, which kept hundreds of gallons of loogies from littering the streets. Also, taxi drivers started to wear uniforms and the nasty smells in their cabs magically disappeared—many taxi drivers sleep in their cars and with bad breath and strong body odor, the air in these cabs was a cesspool. Third, ugly buildings and entire run-down neighborhoods disappeared. There was a huge smoke stack near my apartment that constantly spewed dark fumes. One day, it was completely renovated with beautiful lights on the side and the top altered to resemble a nice sky tower. All "ugly" or older-looking buildings that could be seen off of Chang-An Street (the main street in Beijing that crosses through Tiananmen Square) were refaced. Traffic lines were all repainted. New parks popped up around the city where there once were decrepit neighborhoods. Flowers beds were planted everywhere.

The China Twist

From the moment Beijing won the 2008 Olympics bid in 2001, the country had been preparing for this monumental event. This opportunity was used to showcase China and its emergence as a superpower. Construction in Beijing was nonstop for seven years as old buildings and communities were leveled for new sky rises, stadiums, and transportation hubs. Many old Beijingers mentioned that the pollution in the city only started as a result of the Olympics preparation. Progress?

The opening ceremony would be held in the Bird's Nest, a name coined due to its nest-like structure. Forty-two thousand tons of steel spread over 258,000 square meters, the Bird's Nest would cost nearly $500 million USD and take four years to complete. One reason for the delay was history. Beijing is located in the Chinese equivalent to Egypt's Valley of the Kings. Incredibly, construction crews discovered many archaeological findings and artifacts as they were digging. In fact, they found multiple archeological sites dating back centuries. Unfortunately, due to the rush of the construction timeline, archaeologists did not have time to fully research each site, and the findings were taken away to be studied. For a country that treasures and respects history, such a rush could only be allowed for something as important as the Olympics.

There were rumors that the Chinese government invested $45 billion USD into the infrastructure for the Olympics, more than double the amount for any Olympics in history. We felt special that Auntie Anne's would take part and open its doors during such important event for China.

We wanted to do a soft opening for the brand during the Olympics and then plan a grand opening event when the games were over. To do this, we first needed to finish up our training. Mike Desquitado from Auntie Anne's headquarters arrived in early July to help out with the next step. Mike was scheduled to be with us for two weeks to do a final walkthrough of the store build-out, as well as formal training on behalf of corporate. Thank god he missed all the fun with the blinding light, or there could have been some major repercussions from headquarters.

From the onset, Mike's presence was both helpful and stressful. Mike could not speak a word of Chinese. So when he was training the employees, Joe or I would have to be there to translate. Regardless, he did offer a lot of insights into our operations; when he was not training, he was walking around the store pointing out things we needed to buy and construction changes we needed to make. We worked around the clock. If we were not at the store for the training, we were wandering through local markets trying to buy things Mike requested. Time spent at the stores required us to be in a happy and patient mood for training the employees. Time spent at the local markets required us to be stubborn for negotiating prices. Needless to say, the whole process was draining.

Carlie was also there with us from morning to night. Fiona and Katrina stayed with us for a few more days after the blinding incident, but it was obvious that they could not wait to get out of Beijing, and they soon left. The rest of us felt drained mentally, emotionally, and physically from the fiasco as well, but all we could do was push on.

As training wrapped up, we started to receive shipments, from food items to packaging. Dealing with startup issues also kept us busy. For example, since we expected to sell a lot of lemonade and soft drinks, we ordered 100,000 paper cups printed with Auntie Anne's blue and orange colors—only to have color from the cups come off with a simple swipe of an oily finger. The supplier and I had a huge fight, as he kept claiming we never specified the requirement that colors must stay on the cups. I wondered what kind of buyer would say that it was okay for print colors to rub off. Imagine a customer enjoying a cup of lemonade and a pretzel, only to discover their pretzels turning blue and orange. I found out later that many low-end cafes did not mind this, since it reduced costs. We found a workable solution by adding a food-safe slipcover, similar to the ones used for hot coffee cups.

On July 19, 2008, we opened for business. Finally! At last! Auntie Anne's was open in China!

But, of course, things could not be that simple.

Where IS everybody?!

The Olympics usually brought an overflowing number of international guests to a host city, lifting the businesses and local economy substantially during its few short weeks. This was how Auntie Anne's headquarters described their experience during Atlanta's 1996 Summer Games.

It was not to be in Beijing 2008.

Instead of inviting people to Beijing to view the games and pump up the local economy, the government's goals were a little different. They wanted to showcase China in the best possible way to the world—through creating a perfect image in the media, and TV specifically. Instead of seeing an increase of people, we started to notice substantial number of Chinese people disappearing from Beijing. In China, non-resident foreigners and non-Beijing locals needed permits to enter and stay in the city. Without one, a person could get shipped out. Usually this practice was not often enforced, but it was being enforced strictly during the Olympics. The unofficial figure had it that over one million (out of the 10 million of so people there then) got kicked out of Beijing.

On top of that, many foreigners who had tickets to the Beijing Olympics were not granted visas. Rumor here had it that the top officials from the bureaus in charge of granting visas were not given tickets to the opening ceremonies. Feeling slighted by the Olympic Committee, they flexed their bureaucratic muscles by using the reason of state security to reject masses of people for visa applications.

We gambled on the extra people and sales during the Olympics, but instead we were bombarded with more regulations, increased raw ingredients costs, and reduced traffic.

Auntie Anne's Opens in China

Finally, Good Marketing

Matt Lauer, anchor of NBC's *Today Show*, asked, "Wen-Szu, it is amazing how Chinese people *love* American pretzels! What gave you and Joseph the inspiration to bring Auntie Anne's to China?"

"Yes, Matt, Chinese people do love the pretzels. We always knew that they would love the pretzels. It is part of our master strategy," I declared on national television in the US. Sporting an Armani suit and tie, I was relaxed, chatting affably to the camera and millions of viewers, and looking like a true business executive.

Then, I woke up and remembered how the interview had *really* gone.

While my first actual appearance on TV was indeed on NBC's *Today Show*, there were slight differences. I was filmed not in an Armani suit, but in my Auntie Anne's employee uniform. I was not sitting relaxed on a couch in the studio, but in the Auntie Anne's store rolling pretzels. I was not shown as a business executive, but an employee.

In August 2008, media coverage of Beijing was frenzied. Reporters and TV producers looked everywhere for materials that could provide a unique angle about China during the Olympics. A friend of Joe's was given an exclusive timeslot to submit a piece for the *Today Show*. She had to provide the content for a three-minute segment, as well as a corresponding article for the website.

The plan was for the segment to air several times during the opening weekend of the Olympics. Given that NBC had exclusive rights to cover the Olympics for US viewers, the opportunity was huge. The topic of the segment was going to be on the reverse migration of Asian-Americans back to Asia. For many Asian-Americans, and especially for families such as Joe's and mine, our parents took on enormous risks to move their families to the US to give the kids a better future. Yet, instead of staying in the US, the new generation of Asian-Americans was taking similar risks by moving back to Asia for opportunities.

We agreed to participate in the piece since it would bring publicity to our brand. We knew that it would not do anything for local marketing, but free marketing anywhere is good.

On the morning of August 3, 2008, a full crew from NBC arrived at Joe's apartment to film the first part of the segment. The crew of three or four brought in several large professional spotlights with meters and reflectors to create the best possible lighting in the apartment. The producer analyzed the place first to figure out the best location for the filming, which was to be done with a boom box-sized video camera that looked like it weighed at least 50 pounds. There were several additional people there to help, but I did not know their roles. Most of the crew and equipment ended up out in the hallway, as they did not fit in the apartment.

We did not know how they wanted to film the segment. We originally thought that it was going to be about how Joe and I quit our jobs to move our families to Beijing for this opportunity. They wanted to film all those who were involved. Carlie was already living in Beijing, but Karen was not there yet. I got ready, dressed in business casual khakis and shirt that I ironed myself that morning. I wanted to look professional on TV. I hurried upstairs to Joe's apartment.

The producer had Joe and Carlie sit on their couch, well-positioned in between all of the spotlights and lighting props. I waited eagerly in the room, but the producer asked me to step out to the hallway for a few minutes. The filming was over quickly, in ten minutes or so, and the crew was disassembling the equipment when I was allowed back in the room. The producer pulled me aside. "Wen-Szu, please bring your Auntie Anne's uniform and hat, and we will get good shots of you and Joe at the store."

It made sense that they wanted to film us at the store. I quickly went downstairs to change out of khakis and shirt, folding them to keep the perfect creases I had labored to create that morning.

We arrived at the store as the crew was starting to set up the equipment. Mall security stopped us, as media coverage in China was protected and required permits and prior approval. We informed them that we were filming our own store and nothing else, but security still made us apply for permission on the spot at property management.

The producer surveyed the store layout to figure out the best shot, then had Joe and me go behind the counters to start making pretzels while chatting to each other. The cameraman filmed from the perspective of both the customer outside the store and the employee behind the counters. The filming was lighthearted, as the cameraman just followed us as we rolled pretzels for 10 minutes.

Then, the producer took Joe and I aside for interviews while we stood in front of Auntie Anne's brightly lit logo. The producer had us answer bunch of questions, and the process took no more than fifteen minutes. They invited us to the NBC studio to view the piece live on the opening day of the Olympics.

We were excited that we were going to be on national TV in the US, and we told many of our friends and family members to watch. On the morning of August 9th, the first day of the Olympic competition, our segment aired.

I thought that the segment was very well done, though different from what I expected. I was impressed that the anchor for the story never showed up or talked to us in person—in fact, we did not know who the anchor was at the time. Our footage was cut and pasted into her introductions throughout the segment. And while it was a great promotional piece, I was also disappointed that I had been cut out. Instead of focusing on Joe and me, the segment was focused on Joe and Carlie moving to China (maybe because I was not as photogenic as she is). My interview in the full Auntie Anne's uniform did show up, but only for about eight seconds towards the end of the segment.

At first, my parents were puzzled why they did not see me in the segment. When they did, they laughed at me and said I looked like an entry-level employee. As if that was not humiliating enough, the accompanying online article had a line that read, "Auntie Anne's in China was started by an Asian-American couple." My friends had a good laugh asking when Joe had left Carlie for me.

My ruffled ego aside, the response to the segment was immediate and positive. Friends we had lost touch with, and even strangers, wrote to congratulate us. Auntie Anne's corporate was thrilled, since it was free advertising on primetime TV. Though my first appearance on national television was nothing like I had dreamed, I was ecstatic that the segment had reached millions of people in the US

About a week after the *Today Show* filming, we were contacted by another NBC news show. They immediately came in and filmed the operations, and asked us basic questions about why we opened in Beijing, and most importantly, "Why pretzels?" Supposedly, that segment aired in around 20 markets through the US, but I never saw it. The reporter never sent us a copy, but we were happy for the extra marketing and attention.

As for local coverage, the landlord for my apartment happened to be an anchor for the English Channel on China Central TV 9. All of the TV stations in China were controlled by the government, so the official set of stations goes from CCTV-1 to CCTV-19, with the content ranging from channel to channel. CCTV-9 was the only foreign language channel, and it was dedicated to English programming; supposedly, 60 million viewers watch it. My landlord offered to have us on his TV show to introduce pretzels to the Chinese people. The show would air right before the Olympics started, so it would be pretty good coverage.

Stupidly, we turned it down. We were nervous that because we did not have our business license yet we would be drawing unwanted attention to our brand and our store at a time when everything was so strict. In hindsight, the English Channel show would not have drawn any interest from the SAIC or Health Bureau because the people who enforced these regulations most likely did not speak English or watch CCTV-9.

During the Olympics in Beijing, there was an overwhelming demand for all newsworthy angles relating to Beijing and foreigners in Beijing. Over the years, we were still approached by a few Chinese food shows, but nowhere near the number of times as during the Olympics.

Drip 4

How to Operate a Chinese Business

Locations

Going back to school. That was how I felt with every location we signed. There were always issues, and many related to China.

Imagine a street with thousands of people walking not through a mall, but around it in the bone-chilling cold of winter, knowing full well that they were avoiding a well-heated space. This displays the mentality of the people in Beijing in early 2008: they suffered the cold because they were not used to visiting malls; many of them considered malls to be places for rich people.

The first Western-style mall in Beijing opened in 2001 at the Oriental Plaza, so the mall culture was still not pronounced when we showed up. Over fifty malls sprouted up overnight in Beijing around the time of the Olympics. Most were very well-designed and housed many top international brands, yet no one seemed to care.

Ask any retail person to identify the most important criteria to success and most will answer "location, location, location." Sounds straightforward, but finding good real estate was anything but. This search taught us key lessons on how things were done in China.

Although malls were popping up everywhere towards 2008, customers in new malls were sparse. A brand could get a "great" location in a new mall, but that was no guarantee for success. Most malls needed a few years to mature. Often, the lease only lasted for one or two years for small food businesses, making it almost guaranteed that the stores would lose money for the entire term of the lease. Top brands could rely on their other profitable stores and their brand names to last, but small locations were doomed from the beginning.

Did that cause the rents to decline?

Nope. Beijing was deemed a "must-have" market for many brands, so rental prices grew by ten to twenty percent per year. As we experienced the real estate bubble in the US, we were in for one in the Beijing retail market as well. The rental rates kept skyrocketing. People did not care they were losing money as long as they got the brand name out there. We fell into the same trap, and started opening in new malls.

Then we learned to select malls only with reliable and honest property management, and that limited our selection pool even more.

"This thermostat must be changed. It is not within our guidelines," Mr. Fu said to our contractor, Mr. Pang. Mr. Fu was the property management's in-house electrician and the person in charge of approving our construction at the Gate Mall, our first store.

"What do you mean? This is the same brand and model as the one that was listed on your specifications!" Mr. Pang responded. We had specifically asked for a detailed list of construction requirements from property management prior to starting. Now, in the approval phase, new requirements started appearing.

"No, we must install it ourselves. It's the rules. Without it, I cannot approve and you cannot open," Mr. Fu said. "By the way, you need to pay for it in cash."

"Can we get a receipt from the office for the charges?" Mr. Pang asked, trying to figure out who will finally receive this cash.

"No. You just pay me and I can write out on a sheet of paper that you paid but cannot issue a fapiao (government approved receipts)," Mr. Fu answered bluntly. The answer made it clear that the money would go into his pocket and not to the property management. Of course, their exact same model and make of the thermostat cost ten times as much as what our contractors paid.

The procedures of this property management were setup so that there were long lists of people who must approve final construction before they allowed us to open. Any missing approvals would delay our opening, which would also subject us to fines for not opening on time. Mr. Fu took this opportune time to make some extra cash for himself. The majority of the time we felt stuck, and paid to keep the schedule intact.

This property management advertised Western management practices, including having many procedures in place. When we complained about these last minute demands from many of their own department, the bosses ignored it. So, unless the location was amazing, we tried to work only with international property management firms.

The most valuable lesson was in the art of negotiations, China style. For this lesson, let me introduce Yu Liang, nicknamed "Yul."

"Let me give you a tour of my office!" Yul welcomed Joe and I with a big smile when we walked into a three bedroom apartment, converted into his office. The apartment had all the fittings of a normal office: cube-like tables, file cabinets, a kitchen area and a corner office for the boss. Yul made quick introductions to his staff before we were ushered into his office. The office had books shelves and a big desk, yet the most notable feature of the office was the framed pictures and plaques everywhere, covering all of the walls and on most surface area of the shelves and desk. Pictures of Yul shaking hands with people I did not recognize and plaques of awards, certificates and diplomas.

"Here is a picture of me with the ambassador," Yul explained. "The ambassador and his family are good friends of mine." Having worked at the US embassy in the past, Yul had a good network within the embassy. Yul continued to introduce the people in other pictures, trying to impress us with this vast network. Yul is perhaps the biggest and most aggressive self-promoter I have ever met. His intention was not to brag so much as show us his credibility by being connected to the people he knew, many of whom were movers and shakers; it never felt threatening. A conversation with Yul was a lesson in listening skills and mathematics; children could learn how to count by following the number of time the word "I" turns up in his sentences.

Born and raised in Shanghai, Yul spent a few years in the US studying and working. Due to his vast exposure to US culture, Yul has impeccable English abilities, though in business he lives up to his Shanghai roots. People from Shanghai carried a reputation of being vicious in business, enough so that this reputation helped to coin the term "shanghai'ed," which means to be ripped off or cheated. Yul was a quick thinker and a smart businessman, shrewd but seemingly fair. He was able to gain our trust through his Westernized style and mannerisms.

I liked Yul. He was easygoing and had a lot of fun stories to share, and we occasionally went out for drinks. Yul introduced us to his friends and his contact base selflessly. His desire for self-profit was easy to see through, and though Joe and I kept up our guard for a while, we slowly let it down.

Yul left the embassy to start a real estate services firm that specialized in helping retail brands find locations. As he had great relationships with the bureau in charge of building and managing train stations, his niche was in leasing space in these locations. Supposedly, he was the person who put a McDonald's and KFC into the Beijing train station and several other train stations around the country.

Our purpose for visiting his office that day was to lock down our partnership terms with Yul, since he had a space for Auntie Anne's in the Tianjin train station. Having been in China for a while already by this point, we realized one difference in negotiation tactics. Verbal agreements meant nothing. In our experience, we often invested significant time locking down the terms with someone verbally, only for the person to come in next day and start over because he changed his mind. In the case of Yul, we wanted everything in writing.

Following a contract to the letter is an American practice that was generally accepted as a rule, and guides how business was conducted. We felt safe that we had a signed, chopped contract to substantiate the terms. Yul had followed US protocol every step of the way, starting with verbal agreements followed by carefully wording the language in the contracts we both signed.

Enforcement of a contract was an involved and costly process. As part of the contract, we gave a security deposit, which Yul was supposed to return in full. Knowing that it would be expensive to hire a lawyer to sue, he called a meeting to negotiate how much he would give back. The contract we both signed was crystal clear that we get it all back, but his action sent a simple message: "make me." Yul essentially deviated in his methods and screwed us.

Our suppliers were always quick to sign any contracts we put in front of them, because if they decided later on that they did not like the terms that they signed off on, their attitudes were "make me." Our local friends later mentioned that when they gave a security deposit to rent an apartment, they had already written off that security deposit in their mind. Why should the landlord give back the money already in their hands? "Make me." The landlords would find some excuses to keep the majority of the deposit, as Yul had done to us.

The "make me" mentality towards negotiations permeated even large firms. There was a large Chinese property developer building a new mall in a second tier city. They had been working with one of the largest international apparel brands to open a store there. The directive from the senior management of the developer was that this brand must open in time for the grand opening of the mall. During the store design process, the brand realized they did not like the location and decided to back out of the project. The developer's middle management was caught in a tough situation where they had a mandate from their top management but no locked-in contract with the apparel brand to open a store for the grand opening. Their solution? Copy the entire store. Since the developer had many malls with stores of this brand, they understood how to design and build the store to the specs the brand required. So, the developer built the store, bought inventory from other stores to sell at this store, dressed and trained the employees as if they were the brand. They were opened in time for the grand opening to appease the senior management. The middle management realized the international apparel brand could not make them close down the store before the grand opening, even if they were infringing on trademarks. "Make me" was the attitude, and it worked, because the brand was there for the grand opening.

The entire goal of negotiations was to define terms agreed to by all parties. Strip away the verbal agreements and even written contracts, what was left? Nothing. If there was no way to enforce an agreement, then the terms mean absolutely nothing. Yul did not mind agreeing to whatever terms to make us happy initially, as his focus was on getting our deposit money. Then he had the upper hand and could renegotiate any terms he wanted. Not everyone we negotiated with operated in this sly manner, but Yul did, and he taught us a valuable lesson.

While in the US the signed contract was considered a major hurdle, the priorities were different in China. Many of our lessons in real estate applied to how we treated our relationships with others. One result was that we were much more careful about paying anyone. Even if I agreed to pay a supplier right after delivery, I usually waited until we started to use the products to make sure the supplier gave us what was promised. We encountered too many suppliers who cheated us with lower quality products than what was promised: uniforms where the fabric in certain boxes frayed, furniture made out of completely different materials, plastic cups where the packages of one hundred contained less than ninety… If we had paid out, then we had no recourse; so we delayed payments to protect ourselves. The threat of getting sued was empty, as they just wanted the cash without causing problems.

Power resided with those who control the cash. As the old adage goes, cash is king. When I first learned this reality, I was dealing with investment professionals and stocks, but I soon found that it could apply to many areas of business.

Marketing

We had ten minutes to go before the promotion started again.

Only a few dozen people had gathered so far. The pushing commenced. Just a few hours ago, hundreds of bodies squeezed against the counter during the first leg of our promotion. People were trapped in a sea of bodies on all sides, pressed tightly, rubbing sweat and body odor off on one another. A simple move of the head would cause you to head butt someone. The feeling was not intimate but claustrophobic, as if you were tied down on a bed with no movement allowed in any direction.

People in this crowd were all blue collar migrant workers accustomed to survival of the fittest—people who pushed were rewarded with getting to the front early. They had gathered for the first installment of our 1-2-3 promotion, where we were selling pretzels 90 percent off at one RMB ($0.15 USD). We had run the promotion earlier in the day, and had planned an hour break for our employees.

The remainder of the day's promotion was about to begin again at the Tianjin train station store, and Joe was dreading the last two hours of it. The following week, we were offering pretzel dogs for two RMB, and the third week we were selling full combo meals for three RMB. The goal was to get people to try out the products.

Joe was stuck in this madness in Tianjin, learning how to become a crowd control security guard. The first two hours that morning had brought an unexpected outcome. The customers were not appreciative of the deal. Rather, they were unruly and rude, demanding that other items be priced as low as the pretzels, yelling at the employees to disregard the clearly marked rule that each person was limited to one pretzel, and pushing one another to get to the front of the line. Our employees had a difficult time keeping up with the orders and dealing with insults from customers. Arguments started between our employees and the customers, and between the customers themselves. Joe was stuck in the middle trying to get everything back in order. The mentality of the customers who bought the pretzels was not to try it to see if they liked the taste, but rather to fill their stomachs for one RMB. They could not have cared less if they were getting a bag of potatoes or caviar—the deal itself was what caught their eye.

Nine minutes left. Our employees looked tired but determined. The rollers were frantically trying to twist pretzels, and the oven door was opening and closing with each new batch. Almond Pretzels were being loaded at full speed into the pretzel warmer.

How does one translate a brand name into Chinese? Chinese people are superstitious and tend to draw significance from each word and each syllable of a name. Coca-cola was lucky: supposedly a translation firm came up with a Chinese name which sounded like the English name but also carried multiple meanings of a tasty, fun drink that quenches thirst. Starbuck's "Xin Ba Ke" Chinese name was created by David Sun, one of the original entrepreneurs who launched the brand in Northern China, and his friends over a night of drinks. Most major firms today hire consulting firms that specialize in translating foreign brands into Chinese.

We decided to come up with the Chinese name for Auntie Anne's ourselves. "Auntie" in Chinese translates into a word that means "maid." In a status driven society, "Maid" Anne's Pretzels did not seem like a good idea. Instead, we focused on a phonetic translation using words that signified the essence behind the brand. "An-ti-an" ("安缇安") was born. The first and last characters are the same and means "peace" or "safe." The middle word means "silky" and sounds elegant. As a whole, the name feels feminine, comforting and homey: reflections of Auntie Anne's as it is known in the US.

There were several loosely translated terms for "pretzel" in Chinese, but no consistent name. We took the opportunity to coin a new term. A "ruyi" ("如意") is "a curved decorative object that is a ceremonial scepter in Chinese Buddhism or a talisman symbolizing power and good fortune in Chinese folklore.[2]" The top of the curved object looks like a pretzel's upper two curves. The other meaning for "ru yi" is "as one wishes," reflective of the power to control ones' own destiny. We named the pretzel "ru yi juan" ("如意卷"). The last character means food roll. When we surveyed people about this name, the response was overwhelmingly positive, to the point that people suggested we name the brand "ru yi juan."

"Eight minutes left!" someone from the crowd screeched.

Our first major marketing decision on the ground in China was how to price our product. This was tough task. Pricing food is often a tradeoff between portion size and listed price. The smaller the portion, the lower the price can be. Though most international markets for Auntie Anne's sold pretzels that were 1/3 smaller than the US version, we saw our employees consume pounds (yes, pounds) of rice per meal. We started with the US size.

---

2   http://en.wikipedia.org/wiki/Ruyi_(scepter)

As for pricing, we had to consider that our raw ingredients are close to double the price of the raw ingredients in the US, after accounting for logistics and taxes. Yet, local snacks are extremely cheap, so we could not price much higher than the competition. We decided to price the various flavors of the pretzels from ten to twelve RMB (roughly $1.30 to $1.50 USD by the exchange rate at the time).

As soon as we launched, we began receiving numerous complaints from customers, strangers, and even friends that it was too expensive. Secretly, I agreed. I could buy fresh baked breads double the size and stuffed with meat for a lower price.

Another drawback to our pricing structure was that most first-time customers only bought the ten RMB pretzels, though the most popular flavors were twelve RMB. What that meant was that most of the first-time customers did not try our most popular flavors.

After a few months, we lowered the prices to a standard eight RMB for all flavors. Immediately, we knew that we had messed up. Our sales dropped, but the number of purchased items stayed the same. Our repeat customers did not mind the higher prices but we were still too expensive for the lower end market. We handed out lots of coupons to capture the price sensitive consumers. By mid-2009, we decided to increase the prices again but maintain the one-tier pricing. We decreased the size of the pretzels once we learned that the employees we had seen eating so much rice were only eating once per day. We felt comfortable and confident that ten RMB with a smaller-sized pretzel was correct for our product.

Seven minutes to go. Our staff stockpiled cups and cups of lemonade. One entire counter was full of cups stacked two levels high.

In the United States, Auntie Anne's had not invested in any above-the-line advertising, meaning no TV advertisements or ads in print media. Most of the marketing had been through word of mouth and through sampling. Yes, sampling was that effective. Remember, I was sold on the brand by watching a few employees pass out samples of freshly-baked pretzels. We tried free and low-priced pretzels to let customers sample our products.

First, sampling. Cultural differences made the sampling process difficult. Feedback from customers was that the cut-up pretzel samples served on a thin wooden toothpick looked like leftovers. We had to change the way we provided the samples a few times, from using premium plastic toothpicks, to making individual bite-sized chunks of pretzels, to using small sample cups to put the samples in.

Second, another major promotional activity we leveraged from the US was the Free Pretzel Day.

Given that it is the longest running marketing event for Auntie Anne's, we thought it was guaranteed to be effective. Again, we faced cultural issues.

We learned that the majority of the customers for the free events were not our target audience. They were the janitors, employees of neighboring stores, and other people who usually made less than a thousand RMB (about $150) per month. Ten RMB for a pretzel represented a full one percent of their monthly salary.

Blue collar employees and lower-level white collar employees relied on cafeterias provided by property management and heavily subsidized by their companies. A typical all-you-can-eat meal was less than ten RMB, which included rice, noodles, meats, vegetables, soups, and even desserts. Chances of repeat customers from this target profile were slim.

Another franchisee mentioned that they held promotional events and charged minimal amounts for the products. They convinced us that the event would attract only those customers who could eventually pay for our pretzels. We mistakenly followed this flawed logic. When our one RMB pretzel event launched, we overheard janitors and others in line broadcasting to everyone that Auntie Anne's could make money by selling the pretzel at one RMB. They insinuated that we were committing robbery at ten RMB, though they were more than happy to wait in line to buy at one RMB.

Our last attempt with a major discount utilized the group sales (e.g., Groupon) hype, where we sold thousands of deals in a few hours. But less than five percent of the customers who claimed these deals spent additional money, and most buyers were already repeat customers. Instead of getting a lot of marketing and new customers, we received more customer complaints that lines were too long, or that certain type of flavors and products ran out.

We had to find other avenues for marketing.

Six minutes to go. Employees pulled steaming-hot pretzels out of the ovens and lightly dipped them in butter. Stacks of pretzels were ready to go into the warmer.

Auntie Anne's ex-CEO Sam Beiler recounted multiple experiences where customers have stopped him in the streets when he was wearing an Auntie Anne's polo shirt, simply to relive the details of their fond experiences with the brand. Customers developed emotional ties with Auntie Anne's, which was a powerful connection we wanted to replicate in China.

Trying to pinpoint specific reasons why customers developed the emotional attachment was difficult.

We tried many tactics to associate our brand with various messages, such as healthy snack, imported US brand, fun snack for children. Yet, the tactics were mainly taglines haphazardly placed on flyers, coupons, and stickers with no uniformity.

We wanted to push Auntie Anne's as a lifestyle brand, leveraging the name of the pretzels, ruyi or "如意," since it means "as one pleases."

The younger Chinese population was becoming more independent and free-thinking, and wanted to express themselves.

Our tagline was to be "我的如意生活," or "My life as I wish it to be." We found physically attractive role models with personal accomplishments that our target market would find inspirational: people from top universities, from prestigious firms, and with amazing talents. The marketing campaign highlighted these individuals, with information on their hobbies and of course, their favorite Auntie Anne's snacks.

"Why do they eat Auntie Anne's?" the campaign asked. Well, because it was "我的如意生活"

Five minutes left. Four. Three. Two. The warmer was filled with almond pretzels. The employees in charge of the registers and the warmers were doing some final stretches. Bakers and pretzel rollers did not get a chance to rest.

Unfortunately, we never implemented the lifestyle campaign, since customer complaints about our lack of appealing food photographs made us realize that we faced an urgent issue. Imagine an odd, circular tube twisted and connected together to look like two ovals joined in the middle. Brownish in color, this tube was peppered with white specks and shined like a plastic toy would in sunlight. Enlarged in a picture, this image does not conjure up mouthwatering, out-of-the-oven pretzels, nor does it even have any resemblance to food. This picture was how we introduced the freshly-baked pretzel. For the fresh lemonade, we showed pictures of blue and orange cups.

The marketing materials from headquarters were very professional and well designed, but they were suited for a market that understood what a pretzel was. The issue was not just with us. The franchisee from England spent thousands of US dollars on their own pictures, the Thai franchisee had a full marketing firm that produced TV commercials, and even the Taiwanese franchisee went through the pain to retake the pictures themselves.

During a visit to headquarters, I was stunned by the old advertisements hanging up in the hallways. The pictures were not of plastic models, but rather freshly-baked pretzels surrounded by inviting marinara sauces, cheeses, flour, and various other healthy, natural ingredients. Auntie Anne's marketing in the US had matured beyond these pictures, but the international franchises still needed to introduce the products to new markets as they had done in 1988.

We needed appealing pictures that helped us sell our products and the current ones were not doing the job. Given how serious we felt this crisis was, we ventured into food photography. Hiring professionals did not work, because they were new to pretzels and did not know how to style the food properly. We decided to take the pictures ourselves.

Little tricks became the key to making the products more appealing:. Spray oil on a pretzel dog made it instantly mouth-watering. Gather blocks of cheeses around the pretzels to showcase the cheese dips. Fake plastic ice cubes were better than real ones for the drinks, since real ice melted fast. A few sprays of mist on the side of the cup created the illusion of condensation, vital for any ice cold drink.

We bought our own lighting box, lights, and camera lens specifically for food photography. In the end, we felt our pictures were leaps and bounds more fitting for China than the ones we started with. Our biggest complaint became that the pictures looked better than what the customers received.

Last minute before the madness. The few employees not busy with making and baking pretzels stretched their necks, arms, and legs one final time.

After a few years of testing out various ideas, our marketing strategy whittled down to three simple tools: aromas and pictures were the bait, and the fresh samples were the hook. These were the basics of what Auntie Anne's is built on in the US, and we wanted to make sure we could deliver before engaging in more complicated marketing campaigns.

Auntie Anne's stores are famous for the aroma of freshly-baked pretzels. Our sales volume was not as high as that of the US stores, so there were fewer pretzels in the ovens to produce the aroma. We started to design our layouts so that the ovens were next to the customers and the smells had less distance to travel. Then, we custom designed a fan that sat on top of the oven to blow the fragrance out.

The process for taking new pictures became a very routine exercise for our marketing department. As for the sampling, we developed a constant rotation schedule to ensure that we were always engaging the customers with samples of the pretzel, pretzel dogs and cold drinks.

"One RMB pretzels!" our employees all said in unison. With that began another long two hours of delivering up fresh pretzels to pushy first-time customers.

Menu

Mala pretzels. Frozen yogurt smoothies. Spicy meatball pretzel pockets. Taiwanese sausage pretzel dogs. Tapioca milk tea. Potato side salads. Seaweed instant soups. We tested all of these products for Auntie Anne's China menu. Like all international brands that entered China, we looked for inspirations from other success cases.

This was not the KFC I grew up with in the US. Colonel Sanders looked as I remembered him looking in the US, with his signature black bow tie, red chef's apron, glasses, and goatee. The sign even said "KFC," but this was outshone by larger words: "肯德基," which was the Chinese name for the chain. The menu bore no resemblance to that of a KFC in the US. The menus were all in Chinese, with no English whatsoever. The featured menu item was not a bucket of chicken but rather a soupy rice dish with shredded pork, pickles, and preserved eggs, called *congee*. Chicken wraps were available, but duck wraps dominated the menus. Egg tarts were the popular dessert items. Black squirmy gelatin called, appropriately, "black jelly" floated in milk tea drinks. To top it off, sodas were about a third of the size of those in the US, and did not come with ice.

On the other hand, step into a Starbucks in Beijing and the menu was nearly identical to that of the US locations'. The stores had exactly the same amenities counter with milk, sugar, and napkins. Even the types of muffins and sandwiches looked comparable to those offered all over the world. The text of the menus was similar, but included Chinese in addition to the English.

These were two extremely different menu strategies, yet both were successful. As opening day approached, both strategies made Joe and I wonder: how would we customize the Auntie Anne's menu for China?

In the beginning, Auntie Anne's corporate did not want us to change the core menu, except for adding some complementary sauces and powders. We agreed. The food business was new to us and we wanted to manage the base operations first. We focused on approving the local suppliers and ensuring in-store food quality.

Food safety was a hot topic in China, as there were too many stories of suppliers and restaurants taking extreme shortcuts and substantial risks to shave pennies from their costs. I took the stories as urban legend initially. Not for long. An employee told us a story; one that he did not find too disturbing yet forever changed my perception on food safety. A few months earlier, the employee rented a small cart to sell snacks outside of a busy temple during a three-day festival. The vendor next to him sold a hearty spicy soup, filled with vegetables and ground meat. The soup was cheap, too cheap, to the point that our employee calculated that the selling price was less than the wholesale market prices of the ingredients. So, the next morning, the employee showed up early to learn the preparation process.

The vendor started the cooking process by filling his giant pot from a small hose a few inches from the ground in the public bathroom. These public bathrooms were unlike most in the Western world. Urinals are communal in that they allowed dozens of men standing shoulder to shoulder to relieve themselves. Hundreds of footprints cover the slightly wet ground, which was soggy from all the people who missed the urinal entirely. Stalls had no doors or barriers, but rather a series of holes on a slightly raised platform so one could see a line of contorted facial expressions of men squatting and pushing. While some bathrooms had running water in each of the "toilets," most bathrooms relied on the janitor collecting buckets of water from the hose (yes, the same hose) a few inches from the ground to flush the toilets and urinals. I leave it at that and spare you from the commenting on the odors.

After the vendor returned with water from the public bathroom, the employee saw him take out baskets full of rotted, slushy vegetables and room temperature meats, and dump it into the pot to start boiling. Our employee was disgusted by the ingredients and asked how the customers could eat that without ruining their stomachs. The vendor nonchalantly replied that upset stomachs would not be an issue, as he took out a bagful of anti-diarrhea pills and cooked it into the hearty soup.

Thus, our initial focus was on food safety with our suppliers and employees. Time well spent, I would say.

Our only new flavor was a popular chili powder based on a numbing Sichuan pepper called mala, because we were not able to find the original type of jalapeños chilies available in the US. We also adapted the cinnamon sugar flavor by halving the sweetness to suit local preferences. Unfortunately, upon launch, we realized that our menu needed to be even more customized.

Walk into Chinese restaurants worldwide, and you would be amazed at the number of items on the menu. Many such restaurants in the US even offered hamburgers, sandwiches, and salads. I recalled laughing at some of the menus, thinking that the owners did not understand that people in the US would rather have quality over quantity.

It was funny how things change. When we first launched with the US menu, the local Chinese consumers laughed at us. They could not believe that we would have a fifty square meter store to sell only three things: pretzels, pretzel dogs, and lemonade. The fact that the pretzels came in eight flavors did not exactly impress anyone; the local bread store had over fifty types of bread topped with meats and vegetables, and its store was smaller than ours.

"You guys do not have enough flavors! Just sprinkling some powders on the same pretzels does not count as new making them in different flavors," became a popular refrain for locals and foreigners, who regaled us with it daily.

We knew we needed to grow the menu, so we looked to our competitors to see what worked. One thing we noticed was that lots of people wanted mustard and other dips offered in the US. Due to lack of demand, local suppliers did not produce or import any of those flavors at the price points we could sell them for, so we decided to create our own menu of eight sweet and savory dips: mustard, sweet mustard, cheese, chocolate, and variety of fruits and fruit cream flavors. A dip bar was designed to showcase our line.

Not having seating space in most of our stores determined how we served the products. Consuming the pretzel with a dip while walking and holding shopping bags was a cumbersome task, so we tried to make this easier with a number of packaging options. "Shake Shake Cup" (trust me, it sounds better in Chinese) was developed by cutting up a pretzel into a cup, adding dip, shaking it, and then serving it to the customers with a fork. The product tasted excellent and it was convenient to consume, but also slow to prepare and visually unappetizing because of the slimy sauces in the cup. Suffice it to say that the dips did not perform very well. But we were not deterred and kept trying.

Soon enough, we discovered a major issue with how we approached the entire menu.

One of Auntie Anne's taglines is "Spoiling Dinner Since 1988." This was apt because Auntie Anne's menu belonged in neither the snacks nor main meal categories. The pretzels were too big to be a snack (even the international ones, which were a third smaller than the US ones, were too large) yet not complete enough to be a meal. Customers would look in the pretzel warmers on the way to dinner and remark that they would grab one after dinner. But afterward, they would comment that the pretzel was too large for dessert. Snacks in China include little crackers, small kebabs of lamb, ice cream, or small pastries. In malls, the most common snack was tapioca milk tea (otherwise known as bubble tea), which had little starchy, chewy balls of tapioca floating in it. Tasty and fun to eat, tapioca provided both the satisfaction of a drink and a small snack. I considered these drinks our biggest competitors in the snack category. Our products were good, but we were trapped in no-man's-land.

For a while, we experimented with going the main meal route by adding more savory products and sides like soups and salads to make the pretzel feel like a complete meal. But the selections were too incomplete to try to make a full meal out of. As our suppliers and operations were not focused on providing main meals, we found the quality of the soups and salads not up to our expectations. In the end we doubled our efforts to keep our menu as a tasty snack. We took a look at the Thailand franchisee, which led in innovation for Auntie Anne's as they integrated the pretzel dough into tasty, distinct products. They created different types of hot dogs, sausages, and meats wrapped with our pretzel dough and covered with various cheeses, flavor powders and sauces.

Auntie Anne's in the US created a product called the Pretzel Pocket, which was similar to a Hot Pocket (think pretzel dough wrapped around some filling, like pepperoni and cheese). The product looked savory and extremely good, and we decided to try selling it. The Pretzel Pocket required a large piece of equipment to flatten the dough and another to create the shape of the pocket. We imported the equipment, but immediately realized that it was simply too large for our stores. But the stuffed pocket idea interested us, so we experimented with other shapes. In the end, we developed our own version of Pretzel Pockets we could create quickly and consistently. Instead of the two large pieces of equipment, we only used a dough roller and a plastic teacup.

Pretzel Pockets did very well initially, and we started with three flavors: ham and cheese, spicy meatball, and chicken parmesan. Priced at seven RMB (about one US dollar), they sold quickly and the sales of other items remained the same. When we adjusted our overall pricing structure, many customers began consuming the Pretzel Pockets as a light meal replacement. We compared the prices of other light meals and somehow decided on a new price of thirteen RMB. This was a bad mistake, and we paid for it. Never before had I seen sales for a product drop so fast.

Sales went nearly to zero overnight. Hoping that it was just sticker shock, we started to discount the pockets heavily using coupons. Sales bounced back a little, but not to what they were before. The experience was an interesting lesson on pricing strategy. Despite our attempts to restore sales using discounts and combos, they never recovered to the previous levels.

Next, we looked into selling a variety of other savory products, such as a cone made out of our pretzel dough and stuffed with various toppings like chicken salad or egg salad. Joe and I did not have backgrounds in food science, so figuring out the recipes was hard enough; implementing them in multiple locations was a nightmare. There were always some issues with these products, from difficult operations in preparation to lack of proper suppliers. Our quantities were not large, so leveraging a third party central kitchen to prepare the stuffing was out of the question. Anything we wanted to make had to be prepared in the store itself.

We were able to sell pizzas with moderate success. Pizza dough was quite tricky to prepare. The pretzel and pizza dough required different preparations that could seem confusing when put side-by-side. Figuring it out and training our employees were not easy.

After trying several products, we realized that simplifying the process of how employees prepared the products was equally as important as taste and price. With this in mind, we developed new products based on preparation processes with which our employees were familiar. One example was the Pretzel Dog in new sizes and flavors. The employees already knew how to make the product, so by using different sizes of hot dogs from other suppliers, we could launch new products without extensive in-store training. In addition to the regular Pretzel Dog, we launched the Jumbo Dog and the Taiwanese Sausage (small sausage). We also added some seasonal flavors, such as the Jalapeño Dogs and others, to complement the three Pretzel Dogs.

We also went through a lot of experimenting before settling on a final drink menu. We were jealous of the long lines from the drink-only stores, frequently located next to our stores. These stores sold tapioca milk teas and a variety of other tea-based drinks, and at price points a little lower than ours. These drink stores would have dozens of people lined up at all times of the day. Their menu had thirty to forty drinks that used three or four base flavors. Their menus did not look difficult to copy, so we created a comprehensive competing drink menu.

Working with different drink suppliers, Joe and I slaved in the back kitchen testing out different proportions for dozens of ingredients to concoct our drink menu. Each drink was made with care, as they each had a different flavor and texture. We even bought ice shakers so that each drink could be shaken individually for a bit of visual flare (that would hopefully attract buyers). However, we also ran into some problems here—we were adding a full drink menu to our already cramped space. The drink-only stores had a space the same size as Auntie Anne's for their equipment and ingredients, but we had to shoehorn ours on top of an oven, mixer, warmer, rolling table, and more. Yet by some miracle, Joe was able to design full stations for the drinks.

With both the dips and the drinks, we learned that going from a lab environment to a full operational environment was not easy. Our employees were instantly overwhelmed when we asked them to memorize how to make the full pretzel menu, how to prepare the new products, and how to make the extra drinks. Though we had step-by-step instructions with pictures available on laminated cards, the full complexity of the menu items started to cause delays and inconsistencies. After a few store visits where we witnessed employees creating concoctions in the designer flavors of too sweet, too sour, and too odd, we decided to reduce the drink menu. We focused on just a milk tea base and lemonade base, but added several easy-to-operate syrups for flavoring. This drink menu was not as flavorful or attractive as our previous one, but at least it was consistent.

In developing this menu we learned an important lesson: Auntie Anne's approach must be different than that of KFC and Starbucks. KFC succeeded in doing this with the quality of their food and localized products, and by educating a whole generation of Chinese to love the brand. Starbucks, on the other hand, priced for the high end consumers and appealed to the status symbol that Chinese people valued. Early Chinese adopters proudly showed off the Starbucks logo on the cups. In the process, they developed a coffee culture. Auntie Anne's had more moving variables because we were testing not only the menu but the location size for our stores. The product could be great but if it was inconvenient for the customers to consume, the product would not work. Instead of focusing on individual food items when we customized the menu, we should have focused on the full experience from the beginning. We needed to understand the overall experience of a customer visiting Auntie Anne's to ensure we provided something that customers perceived as valuable.

Drip 5

Only in China

Between a Rock
and a Hard Place

When I googled Steve Jones, I found a winery owner, a photographer, and a furniture designer, but no one associated with the food industry or China, where Steve Jones of New York & Capital supposedly did a lot of business.

And then, on the third page of the Google search, I found him. I found the guy who, earlier that day and a mere ten minutes after meeting us, had flat-out accused Joe and I of colluding with Martin Fan to cheat him.

I pulled up a black and white picture of a Caucasian man in full suit and tie. He was about six feet tall and a little round in the stomach, but not fat. In the picture, he was standing next to a former US Presidential candidate, who was a Senator at the time. With a round baby face, short dark hair, and glasses, Steve smiled radiantly for the cameras alongside an important-looking Chinese couple and the Senator. The picture was from the mid-1990's and had been taken in Beijing's Great Hall of the People, a place usually reserved for dignitaries and VIPs on visits to China.

The posting of the picture on the website seemed to be against Steve's wishes. According to the online article, when asked about the visit by a journalist, Steve responded, "I am not doing an interview with you, and please do not call me again." Sounded like the guy I met.

Let us rewind to the beginning.

✻ ✻ ✻

The day before, I had received an unexpected call from Christopher Chen, a businessman experienced in the restaurant industry in Taiwan and China. Christopher was responsible for introducing a famous US franchise to Taiwan, and had owned the franchise for years. He had also brought several other top global food franchises to Taiwan and a famous food brand into Northern China. Christopher projects power and respect far greater than his towering figure. When I walked into a restaurant in Beijing with him one time, an employee recognized him as the original founder of the brand in China. She acted like she had just seen Tom Cruise or Brad Pitt and ran around the store, pointing out Christopher to all other employees. It took her another ten minutes to build up the courage to approach Christopher to tell him how much she admired him.

The people who worked under him in Taiwan went on to be the executive management responsible for the successes of the top fast food chains in China. One such person was Martin Fan.

Martin was the Managing Director of a famous US fast food brand in Northern China for nearly two decades, and served as the General Manager for China for several years during that period. He was originally from Hong Kong, and there was still something very

Cantonese about his build and his style. His slim body and short frame fit his posh Armani suits well. However, to say that he dressed well would be to shortchange his careful eye on the details. His glasses were often matched with the suits and ties that he wore. At times flamboyant, Martin once stood out stylishly and confidently by wearing an all-white suit to a large dinner party with dignitaries. Martin talked fast, almost too fast. The heavy Cantonese accent in his English and Mandarin made his speech hard to understand in either language. Smart and quick thinking, he always jumped from one idea to another, which gave us the impression that he was always one step ahead of us.

We met Christopher and Martin when we first arrived in Beijing. To our knowledge, Martin and Christopher started a private equity firm to bring food brands to China. Since our goal was to bring more brands into China, we had dialogues with various US brands about being their partners in China. We discussed with Martin about potentially partnering up. We were proud to be affiliated with this superstar duo that we listed them as a partner on our website: www.cfgchina.com.

Since Christopher had taken time off due to health reasons soon after we met him, we dealt mainly with Martin. The potential deal with the brands we discussed fizzled, and we did not have another brand in the pipeline. Thus, our partnership never took off.

Martin also ran a retail-leasing firm with his nephew, Aaron. Aaron often threw a few deals our way in terms of offering some retail locations his firm had landed. In early 2009, Aaron brought us to a great location in a nearby city called Tianjin. As one of the top locations in the city, the storefront could attract as many as one million people per day on a weekend. We signed it immediately and paid a finder's fee to Aaron's firm. The store opened six months later.

As Christopher had been out on sick leave, I had not heard from him for nearly a year, so I was surprised to hear from him.

"Hi, Uncle Christopher!" I exclaimed, with pleasant surprise in my voice. I called him "Uncle" out of respect since my good friend who introduced us also called him "Uncle." After exchanging some pleasantries, Christopher jumped into the purpose of his call.

"Wen-Szu, I am looking at your website, cfgchina.com. I see that you have listed you are partners with the people who brought top US brands into China. Who, exactly, are you referring to?" he asked.

My immediate reaction was, *Crap, this feels like trouble ahead.* Perhaps the partnership claim had been a stretch on our part, but it seemed pretty innocuous. I kept my composure. "Uncle Christopher, we are referring to you and Uncle Martin!" I replied, with an extra emphasis on the word "uncle." "While you were out, Uncle Martin and I discussed working together on some potential deals. Why? Is there anything wrong?"

"Umm… no. I was curious, that is all," he said, though I knew that it was not the end of the discussion. Then to my relief, Christopher changed topics. We finished our conversation quickly.

"Uncle Christopher, if you are ever free for coffee, please let me know as I would love to catch up!" I offered, though my expectations were low that he would ever call.

I was wrong. Twenty minutes later, Christopher called back. "Can we meet up for coffee now?"

Now I was getting a bit nervous. His line of questioning felt like it had a hidden agenda. As I had nothing to hide, I agreed to meet with him. We met at a local coffee shop and had a very cordial discussion about how we were both doing and about his health.

During this discussion, Christopher revealed that he and Martin actually did not own the private equity fund, that they were merely employees. The fund was owned by Steve Jones, a businessman from the US, who had been investing in China for a long time. Martin had had a falling out with Steve recently, so Steve was looking into all the dealings Martin had with anyone in the past while under his employment. Our names had come up.

We did not know much about Steve, but had heard his name brought up once or twice in the past, mentioned along with words like "super wealthy," "billionaire," and various other descriptions that made him seem like a mogul, and one that liked to stay out of the spotlight.

The following morning, I received a call directly from Steve.

"Hi, Wen-Szu, this is Steve Jones! I think you must know me or have heard of me by now!" His jolly voice was thick with a refreshing American Eastern seaboard accent. "With all that is going on, I think we should meet as soon as possible."

"Well, we are quite busy, but I may be able to set aside some time later today," I responded out of courtesy, though I had no intention of meeting Steve that day. Joe and I had full days planned for the rest of the week.

"Fine, that works. I have a lunch set up at Maison Boulud but will be free after. Let's meet at 3:00 p.m. at the Starbucks on the ground floor of my office building."

Click. Steve promptly hung up without giving me a chance to say yes or no.

"What do you want to do about this?" I asked Joe after giving him a recap of the conversation. Joe let out an audible breath and looked like he had been punched in the stomach. He put his computer bag on the ground and leaned against the nearest wall, clutching his hair with his right hand.

This conversation had come at a bad time, considering all that we had going on. A Tianjin tax bureau agent had called the day before and demanded that our legal representative, which was Joe, show up with a specific set of documents. The same agent had shown up at one of our stores recently, flashed her badge, and demanded free food. God only knew what she wanted this time. Joe was heading out the door to Tianjin with the documentation right there and then.

Meanwhile, we were dealing with other issues. We had new employee policies in Beijing that caused an uproar among the employees, new products that we had set a start date for but had not perfected in the kitchen, marketing designs for campaigns set to launch that needed finishing, late financial reports for the investors, and wives upset that we did not spend enough time with them. The strain was beginning to get to us.

Still clutching at his hair, Joe silently stared blankly at the ground for a good minute before answering. "Let's not meet with him. Not today. We cannot…Damn it, why does all this crap have to happen together? I have to go to Tianjin today." He pushed himself off the wall, and his deflated look started to turn into anger. "No, call him back and say that we cannot make it today and let's try to reschedule for tomorrow."

I agreed. But after the third time calling and thirty rings later, I realized that Steve was not going to pick up. In China, mobile lines do not have voicemail, so leaving a simple message was out of the question.

Ultimately, we decided that Joe would head to the tax bureau, and I would go to the Starbucks. I would show up and be silent, though.

I looked for an American as I strolled through the Starbucks, but saw only Chinese people. I walked into the lobby of the office building, which was connected to the Starbucks. Here I saw a large American barking loudly into the phone, his back turned to me. "Yes! The URL is cfgchina.com. Print it and bring it down now!"

The hairs at the back of my neck started to rise. I walked around and approached Steve. His wide body was situated in the middle of a two-seater couch, right in the crack between the cushions. He wore a dark blue suit, wrinkled white shirt, and red tie, and was very fair-skinned. When he saw me approach, the grimace on his face turned into a big, genuine smile.

"Hi! You must be Mr. Jones. I am Wen-Szu." The friendly smile put me at ease, if only for a minute.

"Hi Wen-Szu! I am Steve Jones!" He extended his hand out for a quick handshake after pushing off the couch to greet me. "Please, have a seat. Let's chat."

I rehearsed the planned story in my mind. *Okay, Wen-Szu. Game time.* I needed to convince this guy to leave us alone. I exhaled hard a few times as I was about to form my first words. "Hi, Mr. Jones, I w—"

"Steve! Please call me Steve."

"Okay, no problem, Steve. I appreciate your call today and wan—"

I was interrupted as a big, tall Chinese guy handed a sheet of paper to Steve. The resemblance to Christopher Chen in size and build was unmistakable, but this guy was a much meaner-looking version. I recognized the paper as a printout of our website.

"Wen-Szu, please meet Carter. Carter, as you may know, was the person responsible for operating a popular US chain in Taiwan. He also brought a popular fast casual brand to China. Carter is Christopher's brother."

Carter reluctantly reached over to shake my hand, and without acknowledging me was somehow able to scowl at me. He found a seat as far away from Steve as possible and stared blankly in our direction.

"Pardon me. Please continue," Steve said, turning back to me but with the printout tightly in his grip.

By this point, I had lost the perfect speech. "Steve, I wanted to say that I am not going to tell you... I mean... I am not going to say anything today. Joe and I do not know what is going on between you and

Martin, but given that we do not know Martin well and do not know you at all, we will choose to not get involved. I hope you can respect our decision."

Steve sat silent and stared at me. It was a few seconds but it felt like an eternity. "Bad start," he said, shaking his head. His smile faded. "Maybe you should hear the whole story before you make a decision."

Great, I thought. I had antagonized him.

"Wen-Szu, you are a businessman, so I am sure you understand where I am coming from. I interact with some of the top businessmen and politicians in China and in the United States. Pan Shiyi reserved me the penthouse suite at the Soho Today development personally. I deal with the Rockefeller family in the US. My reach and connections in China and in the US go far."

Later I found out that Pan Shiyi was a billionaire, and the owner of the largest real estate developer in Beijing. Steve, I discovered, liked to name drop.

"Something fishy is going on here between you guys and Martin. I want to find out the truth!" Steve threatened. "I have invested billions of dollars into China and will spend as much to protect my investments.

"I am sure that Martin probably told you that he and Christopher owned a private equity firm. Did you know that Martin and Christopher are my employees at my private equity firm? Yes, employees! They cannot take a shit without me knowing about it. I own them! They are my kids!" Steve raised his voice a little. A flush crawled up the side of his neck, and began to turn his face red.

"A few years back, I was interested in getting the Auntie Anne's franchise for China. I asked Martin to look into it. I did not get the brand, but I see that you guys did. Earlier this year, I was interested in a great location in Tianjin. I did not get that either. Guess who got it? Yes! I saw that Auntie Anne's opened a store there."

Steve gave me an icy stare now. He picked up the printout with our website and waved it towards me. "Now I see that you are partners with guys that are supposed to be my employees!" His tone managed to be both condescending and threatening at the same time.

"You think that Martin has connections with the Tianjin government to get a location like that? He is using all of my connections! And it seems that you guys are working with Martin behind my back. I am going to get to the bottom of this and find out what type of shady things he and you guys have been doing!

"If you choose not to say anything, then I will carpet bomb everything and dig into everything you have. My team of lawyers at the firm Jun He is ready, as I deal with all the top partners there. I will send a team of lawyers after you against your entities in China, Hong Kong, and United States."

Steve simultaneously surprised and scared me. How did he know our legal structure? I still knew nothing about this character.

I tried to hide my nervousness by not thinking deeply about how vast Steve's connections could be, about how much he could possibly hurt us if his billionaire reputation was real, about how Steve was able to hire two legends in the food and beverage business, or about how vengeful towards Martin he seemed. Instead, I occupied my mind with silly, random thoughts. *Look at the new veins pulsating around Steve's right temple! Or am I seeing things?*

Steve started to lose steam, so I thought that I would try to put up a fight. "I understand your situation. Again, Steve, we choose not to get involved in what seems like an internal issue on your end." I looked at Steve's face and could tell this was not working, so I switched tactics. "Besides, Joe and I discussed the situation and made a joint decision to not discuss our dealings with Martin to anyone, out of our desire to stay out of other people's business. Even if I wanted to discuss it now, I would need to get Joe's permission first. I hope you can respect that decision. We—"

"It's too bad. Because you guys are involved now! You cannot get out of it. You need to pick a side! Either you choose to protect Martin and his lies, or you choose to tell me the truth. I will come after you guys if you choose not to tell me the truth. When can you get back to me?" He paused to think for a few seconds. "Actually, get back to me tomorrow! By noon. Or else."

I had no clue on what Steve meant when he said "come after us." Frivolous lawsuits? Hiring thugs? Sending government bureau agents to come inspect us? I had no clue, but I had a sudden urge to get out of there. "Okay. Let me talk to Joe about how we want to handle the situation. No promises on when we can get back to you, but we will try for tomorrow." I quickly departed.

Fast forward. My stomach had been churning after I found Steve's picture with the former Presidential candidate. The picture was dated. So, he had connections to an US presidential candidate that long ago; god knew what type of connections he had now.

Joe and I spent some time chatting about the next step. He called a few lawyer friends and so did I. I also talked to Faiz, my lawyer friend and our investor. Faiz was trying to calm me down by saying that it was easy to meet with a presidential candidate by donating money. Faiz suggested we should explain that we were young entrepreneurs trying to make it in China without getting caught up in someone else's fight. We did not know what Steve was fighting about, but that we believed we had operated fairly and reasonably. Our wishes were to be left alone to operate our own business. We decided to follow Faiz's advice.

The next morning, Joe, being the more diplomatic and elegant speaker, called Steve and explained that we had nothing to hide and that Steve should be able to understand our position of not getting involved. Nonetheless, we would go in that afternoon and answer any questions he had for us. We would then inform Martin of the conversation so we were transparent to both parties. Our condition to Steve was that he left us out of his feud after our session. Steve agreed.

Joe and I pushed back all of our responsibilities and cleared the day. We then spent the morning talking through how Steve might ask his questions and how to answer them in a diplomatic fashion.

When we arrived at Steve's office, the secretary showed us in. She had to use her index finger on a biometrics fingerprinting system to open the door. I was impressed with this security system, the most advanced I had seen in China. The office was fairly small, with three or four glass-partitioned offices, but it had a contemporary feel. The expensive woods, futuristic furniture, matching artwork, and well-placed plants showed the touches of a talented interior designer.

His secretary led us into a conference room, where we waited a few minutes for Steve and admired the Chinese emperors' outfits hanging in thick frames on the wall.

"Hello gentlemen," Steve started out as he walked through the door. "I appreciate you taking time to come here."

"No problem," we said at the same time, in reluctant tones.

"After our conversation yesterday, I have done a lot of research. I have found out most of what I needed to know already and need confirmation.

I only have a few questions. Two actually. I think you will find them very simple."

Steve did not ask the questions initially, but started the conversation by explaining to us his business model and how he wanted to bring in food brands. This explanation took about ten minutes. This Steve was not the same person who had threatened me the day before; this Steve was very social and easy to talk to. Nice, even.

Next, Joe gave a quick explanation of our dreams in our desire to have a collection of brands in China. By this point, Steve was very animated and interested in explaining the technical numbers behind his business. Our worries faded quickly, and we became interested in intellectual discussions on various brands, business models, and even food science behind the brands that we pursued.

"So, what are the questions that you mentioned you wanted to ask us?" Joe asked, as we reached an end point.

"Like I mentioned before, I only have two questions. First, do you have any current business interactions with Martin for other brands outside of Auntie Anne's?"

"No."

"Second, did you pay a commission to them for the Tianjin property?"

"Yes, we paid a finder's fee of one month's rent to Aaron's firm," Joe replied. Steve was nodding his head as we answered. He looked up at the ceiling silently, apparently thinking. We waited, but he did not ask another question, so Joe jumped in. "So, what is going to happen to Martin?"

"Martin is leaving the firm due to cultural differences, and due to the Trojan horse business he had set up with Aaron. I have such a draconian non-compete agreement in place with him that I do not think he will be able to work anywhere in the Western hemisphere—at least not if he wants to be in the food business or in retail. I will not hesitate to enforce it," Steve explained with pride. "I think he needs to move to South Africa or Nigeria to be able to find employment after I get done with him!"

He paused for a few seconds, then pushed back his chair and started to stand up. "Well, gentlemen, that is all of the questions that I have for you. Thank you for coming in." And that was that.

Similar to many foreigners operating in China, Steve probably had his share of getting cheated. So, it must have driven him crazy to see a trusted, not to mention expensive, employee like Martin betray him so blatantly.

We still did not know the extent of Steve's reach. Joe and I both laughed at Steve's claim to stop Martin from working in China. *By now, I bet Martin has deals lined up to compete with what Steve was doing*, I thought at the time. I did not believe that such a contract could be legal or that it could be enforced in China.

Curious at the outcome, I called Aaron a few weeks later. "Aaron, how are things with you? Are you still in the real estate leasing business?"

"No, I have moved on to other projects. I am now working with a Hong Kong retail firm opening in China," Aaron replied.

"That is great to hear. How is Uncle Martin?" I jumped to the main reason for the call.

"Oh, he's doing great. He left China Retail Capital and decided to take a long vacation. He is in Africa now."

Gangster Employee

"I was surrounded by 20 guys," Du Lei recalled on the phone. "Liang Xu demanded 2,000 RMB or else they would throw me in the trunk of their car, and I would not be going home. He also said the firm needs to pay him another 2,000 RMB next month or else he will come back after me."

Du Lei sounded weak and in pain, sobbing intermittently between explaining what had happened to him. His voice shook, as if he could still break down anytime.

Du Lei was a strong guy, both physically and mentally. This native Beijinger had been our go-to-guy when we needed to communicate bad information to employees. For close to a year, he managed our stores in Tianjin, a city two hours away from Beijing. He singlehandedly faced down dozens of misbehaving employees, managed a situation when one employee was slashed by a knife in a robbery attempt on the way to work, moved hundreds of kilograms of equipment from our corporate dorm to the stores by himself, and talked down government bureau employees blackmailing us for bribes.

Today, he was only supposed to give exit papers to an employee we had let go, a skinny, young man named Liang Xu. He was supposed to meet with him at 4:00 p.m., but Du Lei called in tears an hour before the scheduled meeting time.

✧ ✧ ✧

Liang Xu embodied the worst of the stereotypes about Beijing kids born after 1990—spoiled, proud, and lazy. Liang Xu was fairly tall by local standards; yet skinny to the point I could see the bones of his shoulders through his uniform shirt. He was clean-cut, well groomed and dressed, and had worked in different service industry jobs by the time he reached his early 20s. At first glance, he looked like a good hire for Auntie Anne's.

Born in Beijing, Liang Xu had the distinct privilege of possessing a Beijing household permit. The permit allowed access to the local school systems, subsidies, and other services Chinese citizens from the provinces would pay bribes upwards of 200K RMB (around $30,000 USD) for, as they were top notch compared to those in the rest of the country. As the capital city with hundreds of years of history, Beijing also enjoys rich cultural heritage and unparalleled political status. Given all of the advantages and status of being from Beijing, Beijingers are extremely proud people. Liang Xu, however, took that pride to a new level.

Liang Xu was also a product of the one child policy, a policy that gives rise to the term "Little Prince." Without siblings, he was pampered by two parents and four grandparents and was treated his entire life as the family treasure. Growing up with that type of special care and attention makes it difficult for the younger generation to endure hard work and take orders from others.

When I described this employee, I did not mean any disrespect to the millions of Beijingers who were hardworking, great team players, optimistic, welcoming, and friendly. Nonetheless, compared to the employees from the provinces, we found Beijingers to be the most difficult to deal with.

Liang Xu joined us in early 2011 through a referral by an old employee we trusted. Hiring decisions for the store happened at the district manager level, so we did not meet Liang Xu until after he joined us. About a month after we hired him, Du Lei brought his name to our attention during a weekly operations meeting.

"We need to transfer a new employee named Liang Xu to the Wang Jing store and hire someone else for the Raffles City location," Du Lei announced as we were chatting about hiring requirements.

"Why? Was Liang Xu not hired specifically to cover the gap at Raffles City?" I asked.

"Yes, but he had some disagreements with Feng Xiao Xiao. We need a new person in Wang Jing anyhow, so this will not increase the overall labor costs," Du Lei explained. Feng Xiao Xiao was an experienced manager who had been with us from the beginning.

"What happened between them? Could it happen at Wang Jing?" I asked.

"Feng Xiao Xiao asked Liang Xu to sample and Liang Xu refused. Then, Feng Xiao Xiao must have yelled at Liang Xu to get him to sample, and they got into an argument. Most likely, it is that their personalities do not match." Du Lei explained. Sampling is a difficult job, as it required soliciting everyone who walked by. Inevitably, most of the people rejected the sampler, which could be very demoralizing. Handling constant rejection took a certain outgoing and resilient personality, which Liang Xu did not have.

"I had a talk with Liang Xu on the side and he is fine with transferring to Wang Jing," Du Lei continued.

"Ok, that is your decision to make, Du Lei. If you think that he can work out then you can transfer him. If not, he has not passed his probation period, so we can find another person to replace him," I suggested. Most times, we could identify employees who did not fit culturally with our organization during the probation period. Even when they became permanent employees, they usually did horrible jobs and left on their own. So, it was better for both sides to go their separate ways early if the cultural fit was not there.

With that, I thought we were done with this issue.

"I think that we need to let Liang Xu go," Du Lei said suddenly during the weekly operations meeting a few weeks later.

"Why? What happened now?" I asked.

"Liang Xu started to threaten Cao Qing and the rest of the staff at Wang Jing, like he threatened Feng Xiao Xiao," Du Lei said. Cao Qing was the store manager at the Wang Jing store, and she was among the most docile, nicest employees we had. She was good at leading by example, pitching in to help with many hard tasks in the store.

"What do you mean, 'threatened'? You did not mention anything about that last time?" I asked.

"Liang Xu had threatened to 'beat the crap' out of Feng Xiao Xiao, which was why Feng Xiao Xiao asked me to talk to him. When I talked to Liang Xu, he asked me to take care of the issue, which I said I would by transferring him. Liang Xu felt that he was being disrespected by other employees at Raffles City, but would give me face by letting me handle it. Or else, he suggested I get out of his way and he'll take care of it."

"You should have told us this last time!" I said angrily. Realizing I needed to focus on the issue at hand, I did not dwell on the past. "What happened at Wang Jing?"

"Cao Qing asked Liang Xu to sample and he refused. Then, he started to refuse to do other things that he felt were demeaning. Sometimes, he would not even make pretzels. He would also take double the allowed break time," Du Lei complained. "Cao Qing started to raise her voice with Liang Xu, and he responded by threatening her."

"He even sent SMS to her saying that Beijing is a dangerous place and that she should watch herself when she goes home at night," Du Lei continued. "When I tried talking to him, he even started to threaten me. He felt that I did not give him face since I did not take care of the issue of other employees disrespecting him."

"Ok, I have heard enough. I agree with you. Let's let him go," I decided. "Do you think that he will act on his threats, though?"

"No way. Liang Xu is all talk. He would not dare to do anything," Du Lei said definitively. Liang Xu's probation period was approaching in less than a week. Du Lei scheduled to meet up with him to sign final paperwork at one of our stores at on March 23, 2011—the day he called us in tears.

✵ ✵ ✵

"Du Lei, are you okay right now? Were you injured or hurt?" I asked.

"Yes, I am fine now. Mr. Lin, I had to give him the money. He had people with him and they showed up at 2:00 p.m. instead of our scheduled time at 4:00 p.m.," Du Lei said, his voice still shaky.

"Okay, okay, do not worry about that right now. The main concern is your safety," I reassured him. "Let me understand the situation again. You were supposed to meet up at 4:00 p.m., but he showed up at the store at 2:00 p.m. Were you behind the counters?"

"He showed up alone and asked to speak to me outside of the store, so I followed him. We went downstairs, where he had people waiting for me," Du Lei said with more energy in his voice, apparently shaking off the shock of nearly being attacked.

"So, he and his friends asked you to get money to pay him right then?" I continued.

"Yes, he demanded 2,000 RMB today. I gave him the cash out of my own pocket. He said that he does not want to cause trouble, and that if we give him another 2,000 RMB during the next payday, he will leave us alone. If not, he will come after me again. Also, he will go after the other store managers who gave him problems before," Du Lei said. "Liang Xu mentioned that he has visited all of the other store managers and gave them the same warning."

"What?! He already visited the other stores? Did you check with the other managers? Did he go around threatening everyone?" I was shocked. Letting someone go at the end of the trial period was routine for employees who were not a good match for us. In the past, employees who were let go had been upset when we informed them, but no one had dared threaten us.

"Well, Liu Dong here at the Gate store mentioned that Liang Xu called him and threatened him today," Du Lei said. "I am not sure about other store managers," Du Lei continued.

"Okay, can you call the other store managers to see if Liang Xu contacted them and get me the details? I will call some other contacts to see if anyone has dealt with this situation before. Du Lei, good job handling yourself today. Be strong. We will take care of this issue together."

Du Lei verified that Liang Xu did, indeed, go to the other stores with some big guy and asked to see the managers. Liang Xu then strongly "suggested" that each manager should persuade the firm to fulfill his requests, "or else."

The fact that this incident had reduced one of our toughest managers to tears made me believe that physical violence was a real threat. After briefing Joe on the topic, we sought out advice from several friends who we thought might have dealt with this situation before. Unfortunately, no one had, and the advice they offered were things I doubted they would do themselves. The most common advice we received was that we should hire some thugs to go permanently injure or beat the hell out of Liang Xu, and his family as well, if necessary.

Uh, yeah.

Maybe I was naïve, but how did one go about finding thugs. Google? Monster.com? The Chinese Yellow Pages? Ask the local security guard or police whom they've arrested lately? Hiring thugs was easy to suggest. Putting them on the payroll is another story. For one thing, how would you itemize it?

We debated the qualifications for a thug, and the job responsibilities. Nothing too violent, we thought, just slap Liang Xu around a bit and perhaps leave a few bruises. Our search process was short and unsuccessful. The most useful referral was a hotline (which was simply a mobile number) for Dongbei guys. For this hotline, the customer only needed to specify the number of muscle guys needed, and some typical logistical information like time and location. Due to the quantity of people from Dongbei in Beijing (Dongbei is close by), this network spanned every neighborhood in Beijing. Supposedly, the hotline could almost guarantee that its guys responded faster than the police. However, the Dongbei guys were hired to intimidate. Since Beijing was still the capital, security was much tighter here than in the rest of the country. The Dongbei guys did not throw the first punch, to avoid jail and hefty fines. For that reason, the hotline failed our criteria for someone to slap Liang Xu around.

We could not believe we were even having this kind of conversation.

Another option, which I thought interesting, was getting a few guys who could follow Liang Xu for a week. The service was offered by another hotline. We could simply call and order the number of people we wanted. We were warned not to inquire into the backgrounds of the service providers, and told that we probably did not want to know. These guys worked by the week, though I never could figure out if it this meant a business week of five days, or a calendar week of seven days. One guarantee was that Liang Xu would definitely know that he was getting followed, but the big, intimidating guys would not approach or communicate with him directly.

One well-connected friend allegedly did have contacts to the triads (the Chinese mafia). He said that if push came to shove, his contact could make Liang Xu disappear. The cost would be astronomical, and he cautioned us to think hard before we decided to dance with the Devil. Needless to say, we did not even consider that option.

The most sensible option was to find contacts in the biggest mafia in Beijing—the police department. The police department, based on our knowledge, was not very effective unless one has connections. There were simply too many disputes and other troubles going on in a city of 14 million for the police to take an active role in a case of threats with no physical evidence. Word had it that if we knew people in the police department, the police could be persuaded to expedite the cases and assign officers.

The whole scenario was weird, especially from a business stand-point. Economically speaking, we knew we should figure out the expected value of each option's liabilities. Paying Liang Xu off could give him more confidence to come back for more, so that involved a major risk. Hiring someone to take care of him would be costly and might spur retaliatory actions—plus, it was a bad idea. Calling Liang Xu's bluff placed our managers in serious danger of physical harm and might lead to good employees quitting. Reporting to the police sounded good if they actively responded by questioning Liang Xu, but we did not know if we could get them to do that.

In the end, we found some people who knew a detective in the district where Du Lei was threatened. We decided to report this case the following morning and hoped he could help. We coordinated with Du Lei to meet outside the police station.

✵ ✵ ✵

Taking a long drag on a cigarette, Detective Zang slowly angled his head towards the ceiling and blew out a long stream of smoke as he pondered Du Lei's story. He was not the detective who had been referred to us, but we still hoped he would help.

We were sitting in a short, narrow room right inside the front doors of the police station. The room was set up like a monitoring station, with many TV screens and video feeds from cameras pointed at the front of the police station. One other police officer watched the monitors, also with a cigarette in hand. The room was hazy with smoke. Joe, Du Lei, and I were sitting on rolling chairs pulled from the monitor stations. Occasionally, I had to cover my face with my shirt to spare my lungs.

"Tell me again, why did you give him the money?" Detective Zang asked.

"He had people with him and they threatened to take me hostage," Du Lei explained.

"Ha!" Detective Zang chuckled. "But you were in the middle of a shopping mall! Are you telling me that they could have carried you from the middle of the mall to their cars? Okay, okay...so, how many people did he have with him?"

"Well, they had twenty people upstairs waiting. Downstairs with me, Liang Xu brought one other big guy," Du Lei said, with a new piece of information he had not given us the night before.

"Hold on, hold on... are you telling me that he only had one guy with him?"

"Uuhh... Well... I guess, but... but... he had more people upstairs. He... he answered a call and instructed his people not to come down," Du Lei defended.

Joe lowered his head and covered his face with his hand, shaking his head.

"So, if the guy said that he had two hundred guys upstairs and wanted 20,000 RMB, you would believe him and give him the money?" the detective asked. "You are from Beijing! Do you not have any friends that you can call as well? What kind of a man are you?"

Du Lei sat in embarrassed silence. He was beginning to realize the absurdity of his story. "Yes, I am from Beijing and of course I have friends here." Du Lei then pulled his mobile phone out of his pocket. "But this guy has threatened our other employees as well. I have evidence! He sent one manager many threatening messages."

With cigarette and Du Lei's phone in hand, Detective Zang used his thumb to flip through the messages that one manager had forwarded to Du Lei. "This is not evidence," Detective Zang promptly concluded. "Telling someone to watch their back is not evidence of violence or potential violence. You need more than this. Do you have this guy on a recording threatening you? Do you have a video of the people hitting you? You did not even get hit and you are complaining?"

We sat there, stunned at the turn of events. We were not expecting this type of apathy.

After stubbing out the cigarette in an ashtray, Detective Zang leaned forward and patted Du Lei on the knee. "Do not worry, kid. This Liang Xu is a punk and he would not do anything to you. Go back to work like normal. If he hits you and you get injured, come back. If you can get him on recording, show that to us. Otherwise, you have nothing to worry about." With that, the detective stood up and started to walk us out. "Do not worry, he would not cause trouble. I am sure of it. I see hundreds of these cases a month."

We were booted from the police station with no official record of our complaint and with no promise of help of any sort.

Liang Xu's deadline for the payment was on our company-wide pay-day, which was ten days away. So, we felt time was on our side to figure out our next steps. Detective Zang had made us feel like we had taken the situation too seriously. Since we did not want to hire contractors to take care of him, our only option was to see what would happen. So, as a group, we decided to wait.

✽ ✽ ✽

Eight days later, all of our managers' phones started ringing off the hook with calls from a common number. The calls were short and the message clear.

"You better get your bosses to pay up or else!" Then the caller would hang up. We all knew it was Liang Xu, but the number was not the one he had listed in our records. Our managers were obviously terrified. They complained to Du Lei, but no one approached Joe or me to discuss the matter.

As a company, we could not pay Liang Xu's demands or else he would come back. Employees often approached us with reasons on why we need to pay them more, especially if they had leverage against us. We did not want to set a precedent that we would give into this pressure. I knew we took a risk of a violent crime against our employees but we did not want to show weakness. It sounded horrible, but it was a risk we had to take.

As extra precaution, because of the threats from Liang Xu, we provided training to the staff on personal safety, teaching our employees and managers how to become more aware of their immediate surroundings. We encouraged them to leave work with someone else or walk through public areas when they did. We also asked them to call the police if anyone saw anything suspicious or if Liang Xu showed up at the store. Though we tried to work with the mall security, they simply pushed the issue off as internal to our firm and referred us to the police should something happen.

The managers were scared by the constant harassment and did not have confidence in our ability to protect them. On payday, all of the managers either called in sick or did not report to work. Most managers called in sick for at least three days. One manager took the opportunity to call in sick and then used other reasons to remain on sick leave. She did not return to work for an entire year.

Du Lei, to his credit, did show up for work on that day. We showed our support by going to all the stores to call Liang Xu's bluff. Personally, I would have loved to run into Liang Xu—in the safety of the mall, that is. That day, Du Lei was jumpy, always looking over his shoulder. His typical smile was replaced with an apprehensive look. While we were there, he received several threatening phone calls. He was scared even to go to the public bathroom.

The day passed without much incident. The next few days were filled with the same anxiety. We visited the stores much more frequently and needed to help out with some of the scheduling since the managers had all disappeared. But as the days passed and nothing happened, we realized that we had successfully called Liang Xu's bluff. He disappeared and did not show up again.

The policy for store hires changed after this experience. Now, the candidate had to be interviewed by several people, regardless of who recommended him or her. Also, for the most part, we participated in at least one round of interviews to make sure we did not end up with another Liang Xu.

Our Robin Hood

The story of Robin Hood is the tale of a franchisor/franchisee relationship gone bad. King Richard was the franchisor who owned all of England; Prince John was the master franchisee controlling certain counties, such as Nottingham; and the Locksley family was the sub-franchisee[3]. Disagreements over the high "franchise" fees, among other issues, led Prince John and the Locksley family to fight against each other.

In our case, we were Prince John dealing with the Locksleys—only we were the good guys.

Our business model for growing Auntie Anne's in China was based on having franchisees to help expand the brand into each region. There were simply too many regions, cultures, dialects, and necessary local connections for us to accomplish this alone. We thought we would create the model in one region, prove that it worked, and then focus on selling franchises to cover other areas. Our focus would be on quality control and managing raw materials than worrying about the direct management of our own stores. This was the approach that Auntie Anne's used to expand in the US without a lot of investment money.

3   Franchising - The How To Book, Lloyd Tarbutton

We signed our first franchisee in Dalian in 2009 to a young couple. The wife wanted to quit her job to do something entrepreneurial. She was open minded, smart, and willing to listen. She knew that working with us meant a lot of trial and error in how we would manage the franchise, so we had the same expectations. Our training manager spent two weeks in Dalian to help them launch with smooth operations.

Locksley entered our lives later that year. He started inquiring about franchise opportunities earlier in 2009 after his vacation to Thailand, where he was introduced to Auntie Anne's. Locksley was the Chief Operating Officer for a mid-sized IT firm and was one of the early investors in a successful IT startup in southern China. Locksley and his wife went to respectable Chinese colleges. Their upper middle class lifestyle allowed them the privilege to travel abroad, spend time with their daughter, own multiple homes, and drive nice cars. The "perfect" family often seen in Chinese advertisements was a young, good-looking couple with an adorable child and two sets of cute grandparents in the background. Look at that family, and you'll see the Locksleys.

Wearing glasses, and often dressed in a preppy sweater over a collared shirt, Locksley looked like the IT executive he was. His wife was pretty and well-spoken, and worked in the real estate industry. Both of them could communicate a little in English, enough to read, write emails, and conduct simple conversations. I considered them Western in thought process and style, which was why I was intrigued by their application.

So the conversations and negotiations with Locksley began. At this time, we were inexperienced in managing a franchisee, with only the young couple in Dalian as experiment. Although we had gained some experience with the Dalian franchisee, we still required more learning to manage and support a franchisee properly. Negotiating the terms was not difficult, but we were not sure how to support the franchisee properly: how to share our marketing campaigns, how to share new product development, and how to ensure quality control over the products and service. We wanted to build towards hiring a full team to support the franchisees, but wanted to learn the best processes to do so first. We learned from trial and error with the Dalian franchisee and wanted to continue the learning process with Locksley.

Locksley dreamed of controlling the franchise rights of a brand in Suzhou and surrounding cities. Given that Joe and I had learned that building a brand required heavy investments as well as time to get customers to accept the brand, I was very upfront with Locksley. I told him bluntly that he would need to build multiple stores in a short span of time to make the overhead costs worthwhile, that he would most likely lose money overall as the brand matured, and that his most important goal would be to focus on the quality of the product and service. During the initial stages of discussion, he was completely in agreement.

Locksley had grand plans of starting with a café-style store, with a front and back kitchen that also sold ice cream and offered full barista service—a café that would be designed by a well-known Japanese architect in Suzhou. He had visions for uniforms and service management of his staff. He also showed us that he could back up his ideas with action by poaching a store manager from Costa Coffee and partnering up with a head bakery chef from a five-star hotel, as he wanted to assist in the research and development for customizing products to Chinese consumers in the future. Locksley's vision and energy was perfectly in line with what we were looking for, and we loved it.

After six months of negotiations and discussions, we signed a contract. That was the precise moment the trouble started.

Months earlier, we had visited Suzhou to walk through the details about equipment and construction. After one week of intensive on-site training in Beijing for the management staff of the Suzhou franchisee, we sent an instructor to monitor the training and setup process. As soon as the trainer touched ground, he reported many discrepancies of the equipment and construction than what we required during our initial conversations. When I broached the subject, the franchisee reacted by complaining about everything. Locksley said he did not have enough information on the equipment list, though I provided him with full model numbers, suppliers, and even a list of the prices that we paid. The pretzel mix was too expensive, though we proved that we did not mark it up one cent from our purchase price. We had explained the pricing early in our discussions. But Locksley was our customer, so I wanted to provide top-notch service despite the complaints.

Then came subtle hints that Locksley had started defying the rules set by headquarters and by us. From the beginning, Joe and I followed what Auntie Anne's told us to do. We used approved vendors for equipment, followed tested processes for product development, and stayed true to the brand image guidelines. We thought everyone would do that if they purchased a franchise. As we were many times in China, we were wrong.

Locksley and I worked together and planned out the opening, even inviting out Luisa, an official headquarter representative, for the grand opening. We showed up early to help with the launch. What we discovered shocked us.

Although Locksley had ordered a small amount of pretzel packaging from us, we found out he had locally sourced most of his own packaging, using cheaper material and a cheaper printing quality to save a few cents. Moreover, even though we prescribed specific equipment such as ovens and dough mixers, Locksley purchased what he wanted without our knowledge.

"Locksley, what is that equipment for?" I asked as I looked at a machine in the back kitchen. The machine was roughly twice the size of an industrial copier machine, and had a conveyor belt and some stainless steel devices on top.

"Oh, it's nothing. It is a piece of equipment for the future if we ever develop new products. We will not use it anytime soon. But since it is so big, we need to move it in now or else it will not fit through the door later," Locksley assured us.

The equipment turned out to be an industrial pastry maker, capable of making hundreds of pastries an hour—not exactly something that made sense to use in a single, small café. Then, of course, there was the fact that Auntie Anne's required no such equipment and probably never would.

"Didn't we confirm you will use the Hobart brand mixer? Why are you are using a local, unapproved brand?" I continued, suddenly feeling both worried and annoyed. Locksley mumbled a few unrecognizable sentences and then wandered out of the room, as if he had suddenly heard someone call his name. I continued looking around, and things got worse. Locksley made several changes to the overall purchase list we had specified. Our set of approved equipment, from the mixer to oven, had been tested together to ensure the same tastes globally. Any changes will invariably affect the taste and texture of the pretzel. In the end, Locksley complained that our Pretzel Mix was bad, and that the process must be wrong, since the pretzels did not taste the same. Apparently, his commitment to quality control had just been talk. Once he realized that providing high quality products entailed financial investment, he decided that saving money would somehow be smarter.

Thankfully, Lusia was there to support us. I considered Lusia a big sister, as she was the first official Auntie Anne's representative I met. Lusia was Chinese-Indonesian, and at that time had been living for years in Singapore as both a part owner and company employee. She had been our counselor and mentor through hard times, as she had ample experience in opening up multiple Asian markets for Auntie Anne's. Thankfully, she rolled up her sleeves and was able to ensure that the pretzels were top-notch quality by opening day.

At first, we were willing to ignore the transgressions in purchasing small wares and the bizarre appearances of non-essential, industrial-grade equipment, because they had not permanently affected the quality of the pretzels—and because sometimes these experiments and minor infractions could lead to innovations. What a mistake. By turning a blind eye, we established precedence that made Locksley think he could ignore us.

The store did very well in terms of sales and quality control on that first day. Products came out slowly, but the quality was good. We were all in the back kitchen helping to train the new staff and to make the pretzels, with Lusia, Joe and I all in uniform. We were proud of the store and thought they were off to a great start.

The day after opening, we visited the store again and overheard the cashier talking about the curry puffs they had sold the night before. Curry puffs were not part of the Auntie Anne's menu anywhere in the world. The large pastry equipment also looked a bit used, and upon investigation, I found bags of regular flour hiding high up on the storage room shelves.

I confronted Locksley about it. Of course, he denied selling anything beyond what we had approved, though he admitted that the bakery chef was in the back testing new recipes. He promised us that he would not test out new products until he had applied and received approval to do so from us and headquarters.

I knew of a popular cookie brand in the US that signed a franchisee in Shanghai, who had signed a great location that was nonetheless far too large—large enough to be a small restaurant. When the representatives from the parent cookie firm visited, that was exactly what they found. A popular American cookie company that sold wontons. And noodles. And soy bean milk along with chocolate chip cookies. The franchisee had overestimated cookie demand, and desperate not to lose money, they became entrepreneurs. They started to add whatever they thought the customers would like and turned the franchised store into a full scale Chinese restaurant with branding as an American cookie company.

How did one watch over a franchisee in a different region? Generically speaking, the process was similar for all major food franchises. We needed people on the ground to visit the stores. We needed to ensure that the raw ingredients used were the ones we specify. Some ingredients had to be shipped directly from us and some could be purchased locally once we approved the suppliers. We needed to stay in regular communication with the franchisees to discuss the business and evaluate what was going well and what could be improved. We needed to have reliable sales reports and customer information. Experiencing this process firsthand was what we wanted, as we knew the devil was in the details. We approached the Suzhou and Dalian franchisees as learning experiences. From there, we would build processes as we figured out what worked and what did not.

Initially, we wanted to send our manager from Shanghai to go check in at the Suzhou store, but she was not trained to be a quality inspector. We requested detailed sales reports that should have been easy to obtain from the store's point of sale (POS) machines, but did not receive them regularly. Each month, we set up calls with both franchisees to discuss business. I served as the main point of contact so I could learn the ins and outs of how they were conducting business. In addition, we looked into other ways to watch over the franchisees. We constantly read online social food critic websites, where customers took pictures of the store and products. Mystery shopping firms were also available, though we did not hire them due to the high prices they charged.

The franchisees paid a royalty fee that was a percentage of their monthly sales. Since we did not have a direct connection to Suzhou's POS machine, we could not accurately monitor their sales. As the months continued, Locksley's reported sales became lower and lower, though his store was ordering the same amount of raw ingredients from us. Locksley had realized that he only paid what he told us, and began lowering the store's reported sales. At one point, their sales reached a low point of 1/3 of what they had made during their first two months of operation.

"Locksley, how come you are ordering the same amount of Pretzel Mix even though the sales have decreased so much?" I asked one day over email.

"We increased our sampling, so we are baking the same amount of pretzels," he responded. One characteristic about Locksley I learned early was that he was stingy and willing to cut corners. Did I believe he baked the same number of pretzels and sampled two thirds of it away for free? Absolutely not. But I had no evidence to confront him otherwise.

Locksley then started to delay sending out sales reports, which made us late in delivering them to headquarters. The reports contained less and less information. Meanwhile, he complained every week we were not doing enough to help customize marketing or develop new products for him. From the outset, we had explained that since we did not collect money for advertising or product development, we could only share what we developed. If they wanted customized marketing, they had to be responsible for it. Locksley kept demanding services that he knew he did not pay for.

At that point, we realized we needed a solid monitoring system. We could not control what we could not measure. Yet, we knew nothing about Locksley's franchise. Not their sales. Not what they were selling. Nothing. Our worst fear was that they had deviated from the Auntie Anne's menu by using local flour.

Our options were to impose a fine, to pull the franchise rights, or to stop shipment of raw ingredients. Fining him was useless, as he would simply not pay. Pulling the franchise rights seemed harsh for minor infractions of the rules. Stopping the shipments of raw ingredients could hurt the brand and pushed him into selling non-approved products. So while we did have choices, none were ideal.

Eventually, Locksley did not have the patience to grow and invest in the brand as we had discussed. We learned that Locksley did not have the intent or resources to build out the stores that he promised, but wanted to franchise to another person from Suzhou so he could collect franchise fees. Although he committed to opening a few stores quickly with his own funds, he approached us with franchisee applications instead. He reached out to headquarters to complain about us, whilst trying to make the case why he should become the master franchisee for Auntie Anne's in China.

In the end, Locksley stopped paying altogether. We decided to stop shipment of raw ingredients, and ended our relationships with him.

We found that we only wanted to deal with larger players with confirmed resources who could deliver on promises. Our experiences with the franchisees left us with many lessons learned (outlined in the Appendices), and ones that we would apply for the future. We piloted a partnership store with a movie theatre conglomerate based on the lessons our Robin Hood story taught us—one that was very successful and prompted many other firms to approach us to setup the same structure.

Drip 6

Beginning of the End

Tripping Up on Chinese Labor Contract Laws

I felt Mr. Zhong's presence before meeting him. Behind closed doors, we felt his deep voice roaring, loud enough to resonate down the narrow hallway leading to his office. Three other parties waited nervously on small wooden benches, occasionally glancing at each other to offer moral support.

Mr. Zhong's voice was coarse and rough from decades of chain smoking, with a deep growly timbre that reminded me of a lion. His two decades of experience as a mediator for the labor bureau involved handling thousands of employees and employers—often in the unofficial role of the deciding judge. The end result was less paperwork and less hassle for all parties, and avoiding full legal proceedings for petty disputes. Although Mr. Zhong had no formal powers to render final verdicts, he learned that a strong, aggressive stance could make people bend to his ways. He thrived on having power over people, and relished his ability to inflict pain or to grant wishes. Through the mediation process, he also learned the fringe benefits of his position. In a case against the owner of a cell phone store I overheard, Mr. Zhong held up his old phone and remarked how he would love to have one of those "i things, the iPhones or something like that." The employer hinted that he would bring a new iPhone 4 on his next trip. When Mr. Zhong met with us, he inquired about pretzels and remarked how he would love to treat his grandkids to these expensive foreign delicacies. Probably to our detriment, I did not offer or give him anything.

Intimidation was the secret to his effectiveness. Yells and threats were great tools, but they had to be matched by extreme calm and gentleness. Nothing, after all, is more terrifying than a beaming smile and over-friendly attitude that could turn without notice into a fit of rage. Mr. Zhong's physical characteristics showed that he was capable of both. His bald head, gentle facial features, and kind expression made him look grandfatherly, but his wrinkled face was also capable of casting deathly stares. The distinct boom of his laughter was infectious, as were his affectionate smiles.

And his shouting was petrifying. Less than a minute after we heard the lion-like roars coming from his office, the door flew open. Two young ladies in their late teens hurried out, both with tears rolling down the sides of their flushed, red faces. Mr. Zhong walked out, staring icily at the two girls as they scurried away from view. He turned to the bench where we were seated, but now with a smile on his face.

"Who's next?" he said in a friendly tone, beaming.

"After you," I responded immediately, as I looked at the tall, frail guy next to me. He had showed up later than I did, but I was not prepared to go in yet.

Mr. Zhong glanced at the guy. "Come on in," he said as he turned back to walk into his office. The guy gave me a nasty stare as he stood up, but it did not hide the fear in his eyes. The door closed and the rest of us waiting all breathed a sigh of relief. I had bought myself a few more minutes.

I leaned back against the bench and reflected on one of the longest weeks of my life.

✡ ✡ ✡

"Let me see if I understand this correctly. So, what you are saying is that even though we have paid our employees on time for the past three years, including raises, bonuses, overtime, and six insurances, they can sue us for double pay since we "took advantage" of them by not having a renewed contract?" I asked our HR lawyer, Adrian.

"That is absolutely correct. According to labor contract laws, after the original contract ends, you must renew within a month. Otherwise, you have to pay double for the entire period that they are not under contract. It is not the same as the US. You guys are foreigners so you do not understand," Adrian explained.

"That is bullshit! Several people told us that if we do not sign a renewal contract, it automatically renews after one month. Also, we asked several of the employees to come in to sign, but since our HR left, no one followed up on it. Is that evidence that we tried to get them to re-sign?" I asked.

"Do you have physical evidence of your notice? Do you have recordings or signed notices from them?" Adrian asked.

"No, we asked them verbally and may have sent an email or two about it," I said. "I know for sure that we did not write it out formally."

"Email is not considered evidence in a court of law here. You need to get it on a recording, get a return receipt on an express package service, or get a signed confirmation of receipt of notice," Adrian explained. "Well, we can fight the charges in court and push the verdict for up to a year, but you will lose in the end. Most of the factories that closed down due to labor problem in China shut because of this exact reason. I am afraid that you will probably have to pay out double to all eight of your employees, and it may run a few hundred thousand RMB."

We were learning the hard way that the underlying concept behind labor laws in China was drastically different from that of US laws. Although we had HR lawyers draft all of our legal contracts, we were unsure about the details and the technicalities of how they were to be implemented. In the US, labor laws were based on a concept called "at will," which meant employees could quit at any time and could be terminated for pretty much any reason outside of anti-discrimination laws. Chinese employment law used a contract employment system, meaning that all employees must be under written contract. Terminating employee contracts was difficult, even with hard physical evidence of wrongdoing on an employee's part. The labor contract law transferred the responsibility of the "Iron Rice Bowl" from state-owned entities to private enterprises. The "Iron Rice Bowl" was the concept of guaranteed job security, a concept that was essential to social stability and the survival of the Chinese Communist Party. In China, having a job was a right and not a privilege.

Unluckily for us, China drafted strict new labor laws that went into effect right when we arrived in January 2008. Some parts that would come to haunt us included the following: employees must have a signed written contract within a month of employment; only one extension of the contract is allowed, and then the employee must enter a 'lifetime' contract (yes, *lifetime!*); termination of employees could only be for cause, and the cause must be clearly documented; there was no such thing as a salaried employee as each employee was hourly and salary must be calculated accordingly; and each employee must receive full benefits and insurance (six different types of insurance that could result in payout of 30–45 percent of their salaries).

What did all of this mean for employers? It meant that labor costs increased drastically, especially when all of the covenants of the new labor laws were enforced.

The main target of the new labor laws were domestic firms (sweat shops, factories, etc.) who were responsible for the majority of wage defaults, forced labor, and other infringements on labor laws. Unfortunately, many of these domestic firms figured out other methods to circumvent the new laws. One restaurateur I knew in Beijing, for instance, had over seventy employees in his restaurant and did not have a written contract with any of them. He operated like the majority of the restaurants in Beijing—on the fringe, only caring about the laws that could be enforced against him. He faced almost none of the issues we faced on the regulatory front. If his employees did indeed cause a scene, he would pull some administrative tricks to close the firm down and open a new one at the same location. The employees would not have the ability to go after the new firm. The tactics seem underhanded to me, but he explained that his business could not possibly survive otherwise.

Foreign firms had better track records than local firms of treating their employees well, but foreign firms suffered drastically as a result of the new laws. Laws that were designed to prevent firms from abusing employees were now used by employees to abuse the firms. Labor lawyers lined up class action suits in late 2007 and started to sue foreign enterprises as soon as the laws went into effect. Local firms, meanwhile, evolved to circumvent the labor laws.

In our case, our employee issues started in mid-2011. We had run into a series of operational issues involving our manager, Du Lei, the same man in the center of our gangster employee issue. We decided to let him go after nearly 20,000 RMB went missing from a store he was managing. We prepared proof that he was in charge of the store at that time, and used it and the police report of stolen cash as proof to terminate his contract. In consideration of Du Lei and that fact that his wife had just given birth, we gave him the option of staying on, but to be demoted for a period of time. The discussions with Du Lei were all very cordial, and he scheduled a time the following week to come in to sign the exit paperwork.

The following week, Du Lei did not show up. We thought he had decided to forgo the paperwork, which was common occurrence with other employees who had left. A week or two later, when we had forgotten about the issue and sent Du Lei's last paycheck, we discovered that we should not have let the matter go. We received a call from a mediator from the Labor Bureau, asking us to report immediately the next morning or face heavy fines. Despite all of the ways in which it had adopted capitalism, China was still a communist country that watched over the common laborers. The Labor Bureau was the one bureau many entrepreneurs fear, as it has the teeth to bite and bite hard.

Du Lei had discovered that his contract was not renewed and found his angle to go after us. He worked together with two other current managers, Zhu Boxing and Zhang Bao, to report us to the labor bureau. These employees would spend the morning working in the stores and the afternoon in the Labor Bureau finding ways to sue us.

As soon as we received the call from the Labor Bureau, we discovered six other employees who had expired contracts. That same day, I prepared renewal contracts and hopped in a cab to visit each employee to try to fend off any additional liabilities. The first person I ran into signed it immediately without saying a word, but then he must have informed the other employees. By the time I showed up at the other stores, I found Zhang Bao, Zhu Boxing, or Du Lei there chatting with the employees. The five additional employees refused to sign. For the first time, they started to use terms like "we were wronged," and started making up outright lies that we had ignored them when they reminded us directly to sign the renewal contracts.

These were our most trusted employees, and more importantly, our friends. We had looked after all five of them for years—giving speeches at their weddings, inviting them into our homes for home-cooked meals, caring for them during personal emergencies. These employees were like family to us, having shared so much of our time together over the past few years opening stores, testing out new products and promotions, and working our asses off to improve the Auntie Anne's brand in China. But once they discovered the loophole in their contract, they completely abandoned us. They unionized.

✡ ✡ ✡

"These guys are smart! Not many people work in groups like this," Mr. Zhong chuckled as he flipped through the complaint files from the employees. He was shaking his head in a sign of sorrow for us. "These young Beijing punks. I am a native Beijinger and I hate dealing with Beijing people. Especially the younger generation ones. They are lazy and rely only on their parents."

Young Beijingers were the worst employees to get into labor disputes with, since they could live at home and refuse to negotiate. Non-Beijingers had the pressures of paying for day-to-day living and could not let this process drag on for months, so they would be much more willing to negotiate and take whatever payment they could get quickly.

Du Lei wanted three additional months of financial compensation, claiming that we fired him inappropriately. To top it off, he claimed that we did not give him proper layoff notice, and he wanted extra compensation for that too.

"I am sorry to say, but it looks like you will be liable for all of these charges," Mr. Zhong concluded after flipping through the documents for a minute. "There is not much that I can do about it. I feel bad for you guys."

"What about the charges of inappropriately firing him? He was managing a store that had 20,000 RMB stolen! Is not that grounds for firing?" I asked.

"What type of evidence do you have?"

"Du Lei is an area manager, but we assigned him to manage the store that day. Other managers were there, but they were specifically notified that Du Lei was in charge. Also, we have a police report for the stolen money. That should be plenty."

"Well, is there signed documentation that he was managing the store that day? A signed timesheet or something like that? Without a written confession or something concrete, you do not have any evidence that can be used to fire him."

"He is an area manager, so he doesn't clock in at each store, but we notified him by phone to manage the store that day."

"That is not enough. Under Chinese labor laws, you cannot fire someone without evidence. My advice to you is to have your lawyer negotiate with them to see if you can settle out of court for all of these issues. It does not matter what 'evidence' you think you have, I am telling you that you will lose."

We decided to follow Mr. Zhong's advice to approach the employees personally to resolve the issues.

Once again, we made a bad move.

The Google Way
Will Get Us Attacked

"You should move as soon as possible!" a lawyer friend from DLA Piper, urged us. "If the employees are upset, you never know what will happen. We have seen too many cases of employers being attacked."

Growing up during the dot-com days showed us startup practices we wanted to experience—slaving day and night with passion to launch the business, sacrificing anything and everything to make sure that we realized our dream, and treating every employee like family. The legendary stories of Google and Hewlett Packard starting out of garages served as inspiration. To be able to accomplish so much yet start so small was a dream that most entrepreneurs held as the ultimate triumph.

That was why we conducted meetings, trainings, and all business activities in our apartments for over three years. Not only did we have employees work there constantly, we had store level employees coming through all the time for meetings. Even complete strangers like job applicants and suppliers were common in our converted home office. Karen and I used a small room that had a separate bathroom, but all the other rooms were common space. Muddy footprints on our floors and the fish bones clogging our kitchen sink even though we never cooked fish reminded us that we had lost all privacy, as did the stench from suppliers that lingered long after work hours. The office was situated at my apartment first, and eventually moved to Joe's apartment, so we both experienced these issues firsthand.

Though it was not ideal, we made the sacrifice for the good of the company in order to save money. However, one of the major downsides was that everyone knew where we lived. I had never contemplated the possibility of our safety coming into jeopardy, but that was precisely what happened when we ran into employee issues.

Our accountant Jiang Ye looked through the peep hole. She saw Zhu Boxing standing by himself outside the door of our office, which was also Joe's apartment. She opened the door to let him in. Instead of seeing Zhu Boxing alone, eight of our employees appeared out of nowhere and barged into Joe's apartment, demanding to speak to us.

Loud, rude, and rambunctious, the eight had coordinated this gathering at the office. Six of them were supposed to be at the stores working at that precise moment. The other two were on maternity leave, each more than six months pregnant. The pregnant ladies complained previously that they could not make it to the office to work due to unsafe public transportation and a barrage of other reasons. We decided to support them and let them take their paid maternity leave early. But they had no problems making this trip. The three office employees felt threatened by the group's aggressive manner, but were powerless to calm them. We were not there at the time. The stage was set for an eventual showdown.

The eight employees were reacting to a notice that we sent out on the recommendation of Lawyer Cai, an attorney referred to us by a family friend of Joe's. He was in his late forties, but the wrinkles on his dark, sun-aged skin made him look a decade older. At first glance, I would have guessed that he was a farmer. Our contacts recommended him to help us battle our employees in labor disputes. He was experienced, they said. Use him. So we did.

Cai offered lots of advice on how we should deal with our eight troublemaker employees, all of which revolved around taking an aggressive stance. He told us to force the employees to come in and sign a renewal contract, or else tell them to meet us in court. He drafted a notice for each of the eight employees to meet him to sign a renewal contract within three days or to simply quit, since our contracts with them had expired. Obviously, the eight people were not pleased with this turn of events, hence the reason for the "visit."

Cai assured us that he would personally meet each employee for the signing. As we still worked with each of the eight employees, we did not want to be the person to meet with them. We needed a buffer so we could try to maintain a personal relationship with them all.

Yet, immediately after sending out the notice, Cai called and informed us that he needed to go out of town for the remainder of the week.

"Do not worry, it is an easy meeting," he assured us. "Nothing to it. You need to present the renewal contract and offer to let them sign it. If they say no, then that is okay as well. Simple."

"Oh yeah," he continued. "Just make sure that you record it all. And a small detail on that. Better not let them know that you are recording. So simple."

What the hell is this? I thought. Now I needed to figure out how to conduct secret recordings? *Was I in the FBI?*

"One last thing. You need to make sure that you get them to identify themselves or acknowledge their names. You need to explain the situation of the renewal contract clearly and capture a clear recording of them saying "yes" or "no" to the renewal question. Very simple. Should be a breeze," he said.

Yeah. A real breeze it was!

We were ready. Over three days, we planned out every detail of our meeting with the employees. We scheduled for them to come in individually over a four hour period on a Friday afternoon. Then we set their work schedules so that they could not all congregate at the same time without skipping work.

I walked around an electronics market and learned about different options for a recording device—options included a recording pen and varieties of small handheld recorders. Quality was all directly correlated to price. Still, nothing looked very reliable. More importantly, they would all stick out and would be noticed. After spending some time googling this topic, I found our solution: iPad and iPod. The employees were used to seeing me carry these devices around with me. Surprisingly, there were many great iPod recording applications built for this very purpose. We diversified our risk and used two different applications in case one was better than the other.

Next, we rented a private room at an upscale coffee house. Our private room was quite small and cramped, maybe ten square meters, rectangular with a couch stretching over two and half sides of the room, and a large coffee table about the height of my stomach. We situated ourselves facing the door, so that when the employees walked in, they would face us with the table in between and could easily sit down upon entering. Joe sat so that he would directly face the employee and I would be on the employee's right side.

Now, where would we hide the recording devices? On the couch next to the employees? That seemed too obvious. If the iPad and iPod were on the table in front on the employees, they would know something was up as well. So we decided to fill the table up with a lot of things, including our laptop, some coffee cups, and little snacks. Joe put a pen and notebook on top of the iPad so that it looked inconspicuous. I had my iPod in a case, so I put the case next to the employees and put my Blackberry on top of it so that it looked inconspicuous too. The process was set so that the employee helping us, Jiang Ye, would go out to get the employee we were going to talk to. When Jiang Ye knocked on the door, she would wait for us to turn on the recording and enter only after we said, "Come in."

The thought of directly confronting each of our old employees was gut-wrenching. Before we started, I constantly caught myself tuning out and staring at the floor, while playing out different scenarios in my mind. We did not have the upper hand, as they were all working together to leverage government bureaus to threaten us. Still, we felt ready for this day.

The meetings were scheduled to start at 2:00 p.m., and we were ready by 1:45 p.m. Fifteen minutes passed, but no employee appeared. We were anxious from the very beginning, but now I could feel the acid in my stomach start to churn painfully around. When we called him, the employee we were going to meet first said that he would be late. We tried calling ten minutes later, but he had turned off his phone. Two-thirty rolled around and still no one showed. The employee scheduled for 3:00 p.m. said that she was on a bus and would get there at 4:00 or so. Their timing became fairly coordinated after that, and we realized that they were all going to show up together. Based on their response, the showdown would happen at 4:30 or so. Our room became eerily silent as we waited through this calm before the storm. Joe flipped through files on his laptop trying to keep himself busy, Jiang Ye reviewed employee renewal contracts to ensure they were accurate, and I played Pong on my Blackberry. We hardly spoke at all

At 4:18, Jiang Ye's phone rang. It was an employee. She left to get him.

"Come in," we said after we heard the knock on the door less than thirty seconds later. We were expecting to see Jiang Ye and one employee, but it was only Jiang Ye by herself, looking panicked.

"All eight people are outside. They tried to follow me in but I had the waiters up front keep them there and I ran here so they could not follow," Jiang Ye said apprehensively.

"Please go out there and tell them to send in one representative. If not, this meeting is over," Joe said.

She went out to relay the message and came back to say that they would send in Du Lei as their representative. We agreed.

A minute later, she knocked on the door. "Come in," I said, after turning on the recording application again.

When Du Lei walked in, Joe was very good in loudly greeting him with "Du Lei, how are you?" and then waiting for him to acknowledge us. So far so good. This might not be so hard after all, I thought.

Du Lei came in all smiles and we exchanged a few words before turning to the task at hand. Jiang Ye handed a renewal contract to Du Lei and we gave him a few minutes to flip through it. He spent a good five minutes looking before Joe started in.

"Du Lei, The Pur-Pose Of This Mee-Ting Is To See If You WanT To Re-Sign This ReNewAl ConTRact," Joe roared, enunciating each word artificially. Joe could not have made it clearer that we were recording this session, but his distinct enunciation brought a chuckle out of me in the midst of this madness.

"Well," Du Lei started. "There are problems with this contract. The beginning date of the contract is wrong, since it should be listed as today." He flipped through it some more. "Also, this is not a renewal contract, it is a make-up contract."

I did not know what the hell the difference was, but I guessed, according to the labor laws, that it was a big difference. Jiang Ye started to say what the lawyer instructed her to say to explain the difference between a renewal and a make-up contract.

"Again, Du Lei, The Pur-Pose Of This Mee-Ting Is To See If You WanT To Re-Sign This ReNewAl ConTRact. Will You Sign ToDay? Yes or No?" Joe kept to the script in his perfectly enunciated speech. I began to think that we should have used a prerecording for this occasion.

Du Lei must have sensed a trap. He continued to ask questions about the dates then started to ask about random parts of the contract. We stared at him, as if we did not know any other words but those in the script handed to us by the lawyer. Ten minutes of the same line of questions passed.

"Again, Du Lei, The Pur-Pose Of This Mee-Ting Is To See If You WanT To Re-Sign This ReNewAl ConTRact. Will You Sign ToDay? Yes or No?" Joe reiterated.

"No, I will not sign this contract," Du Lei finally replied.

I could not believe it! We got him to say 'no' on record. We smiled, thanked him, and quickly booted him out. Jiang Ye then went out to get the next person. Joe and I scrambled to check that our recording worked. It did. The recording was crystal clear. God, I loved Apple products! We instantly felt more relaxed.

As the next few employees came in, they caught on to the fact that we wanted them to say "no" or "yes." They did not give into the pressure, and their responses became scripted and identical. We asked if they wanted to sign the contract, and they replied, "Yes, I would like to sign this contract today, but please make sure that the date is changed to start today. The rest of the contract is okay." For several of the hard-nosed people, the conversations consisted of nothing more than repeating the exact same phrases on both sides, over and over again. We could not get a direct "no" from them, but this was okay, as the recording showed effort on our parts and the fact that they were not willing to sign the contract in its the current state.

As we strategized in the room about how to trap them, the employees were doing the same outside as a group. They wanted to avoid giving us anything of use. Each discussion became a chess game of words. Thank god Joe was very good at it. We chose the order of the people by how we felt they would respond to us. We saved the best talker of the group, Zhu Boxing, for last, as he would be hard to get anything out of. By the time he entered the room, the trap had reversed.

Zhu Boxing looked like a harmless teddy bear, and he played this to his advantage. Naturally gifted with words, he was very friendly and could get people to like him quickly. However, he usually had a hidden agenda. When he was on our side, he was amazing at getting employees to bend to his will. He could convince them to not quit, convince Health Bureau members to forgo fines, and sweet talk his way out of most situations. But though he was great at talking, he was also extremely lazy, all talk but no action. Now that he had flipped sides, he was a nightmare to deal with.

He usually wore thick cargo shorts during the summer. Many people in the working-class population we typically dealt with only have one or two sets of clothing they wore every day. I once praised Du Lei's stylish new shirt, which stopped looking as nice after he wore it every day for four or five months. Zhu Boxing strutted in wearing a long pair of basketball mesh shorts made of thin material. As soon as he sat down, I saw why. He had his phone half sticking out of his pocket. The top of the phone was blinking red—recording. *Holy crap*, I thought. He was trying to flip the game on us.

Things were starting to get interesting.

"Zhu Bo Ying, The Pur-Pose Of This Mee-Ting Is To See If You WanT To Re-Sign This ReNewAl ConTRact. Will You Sign ToDay? Yes or No?" Joe asked.

He ignored our question and jumped into his prepared story.

"Mr. Lin. Mr. Sze," he started as he nodded formally towards each of us in the most respectful manner. "I must thank you for the opportunity to learn from you and the opportunity to be employed by the two of you these past few years. I have and will forever cherish the experiences." His speech suddenly became much more distinct, with each word enunciated clearly. "As You Know, AlThough My ConTRact States That I Star-Ted WorKing In DeCemBer 2008, In Fact, I StarTed WorKing With You Fine GenTleMen In June 2008, Is That Not CorRect?" he enunciated right back at us, with his head turned downwards so that his recorder could capture his words.

Joe and I stared blankly at him. I wondered how we should answer, but Joe quickly replied. "Again, Zhu BoYing, The Pur-Pose Of This Mee-Ting Is To See If You WanT To Re-Sign This ReNewAl ConTRact. Will You Sign ToDay? Yes or No?"

Zhu Boxing made a show out of pressing his lips together tightly and with a mocking grin on his face; he shook his head at us. The conversation turned non-verbal as neither party wanted to give up anything. For several more minutes, both sides tried different tactics to capture the other side on recording, but our chess game of words came to a stalemate. We thanked him and let him leave.

☆ ☆ ☆

"Damn, babes, do NOT argue with me right now!" Joe screamed into the phone he was holding directly in front of his mouth. We were on the sidewalk with thousands of other people hurrying home during rush hour. Constant honking, people screaming to hear each other, and other city noises one expects from Friday afternoon peak-time made for truly deafening noise pollution. I had my umbrella over us both to keep away the light drizzle as we made our getaway through a back kitchen exit.

The meeting did not end after Zhu Boxing left. Jiang Ye went out to use the restroom ten minutes after Zhu Boxing had left, and saw all eight employees still waiting outside the coffee shop ominously. Except that they were not waiting in front of the door where we would see them; they were hiding around the corner, out of eyesight of anyone exiting through the front of the coffee shop. We had spent the past few intense hours negotiating and waiting for the employees, and they were all milling around waiting for us.

What was so urgent? We asked ourselves. But we were too mentally and emotionally spent to find out. So, like thieves in the night, we asked the waiters to help us exit through the entrance typically used to remove trash from the restaurant. We all opened our umbrellas to cover our escape in case any of our employees were outside smoking or looking out the window. This feeling of running to avoid capture was humiliating, tiring, and draining. As we walked, I constantly had the urge to look over my shoulder to see if anyone was following. I realized then that criminals who have spent years hiding from authorities could not possibly be living good, relaxing lives.

Joe quickly realized after we left that the employees could go to the office, his apartment, to look for us right when Carlie was on her way home from work.

Joe immediately got on the phone. "Hello! Carlie! Can you hear me? Where are you? Can you go to Joyce's to hang out until I get back?" He paused for her response. "No! Nothing is wrong! But, still! Can you go to Joyce's to hang out? Actually, go to Jackie's to hang out. She should be home!"

Joe was screaming, his face red and veins pulsing from his forehead. He had only been agitated and tired in the room, but now he was panicked and terrified that the world was collapsing all around him. Jiang Ye and I stared at Joe for a second, absorbing the shocking change in his attitude. Jiang Ye moved a few steps away.

"Damn it, BABES, I never ask you to do anything but please just listen to me this time. Do not go home! Just go hang out with Joyce or Jackie." Then, quickly changing his mind, Joe screamed, "Fine! If you go home, do not open the door for anyone except me! I will be home soon."

Joe paused again. "Please, babes. Just go to Jackie's to hang out." He finally listened to a few words that Carlie said. "I am totally safe! I am fine. Do not worry about me!"

If I had not been with Joe before this sudden change in tone, I would have thought that there was a murderer waiting at the apartment. Carlie must have been panicked from his tone.

Suddenly, Joe's faced relaxed and he calmed down quickly. Carlie must have agreed not to go home. Though it was not the time or place, I became quite amused by his short conversation. This scene reminded me of a gangster movie when a person was about to face the mob boss after getting caught stealing from him. Of course, the situation was not funny at all. Our families were vulnerable because the employees all knew where we lived.

Joe tried to calm down before his closing line: "By the way, babes, can you hear me? I love you! I love you!"

✿ ✿ ✿

We decided to walk home that night. We became very jumpy at any cars that passed us and anyone who walked near us. Joe needed to go meet up with Carlie, but walked me home first to make sure that no one jumped me on the way. The employees were not there.

Both Joe and I planned time with the real estate agent the following day to look at new apartments. We tried hard to figure out how to tell our wives we might need to move immediately. We prepared pictures of each problem employee so we could inform the security guards in our neighborhood we felt threatened.

Though we started taking more precautions, we did not move immediately. We were prepared to if future discussions with the employees did not go well. The discussions on this day ended at an impasse, with nothing gained or lost for either party, but it was not over. We hoped that discussions could continue amicably.

Final Decision

Despite the non-stop challenges we had experienced through the years, we were getting better at what we were doing. Locations opened at our desired malls, menu development became more focused on our strengths, operations became more standardized in spite of the recent employee issues, and marketing initiatives launched based on a quarterly schedule. We served regular catering accounts and repeat customers. From ground up, we developed and implemented detailed processes around all parts of our business that guided the day-to-day management.

By early 2011, our stores had reached break-even on a per-store basis. We had two franchisees and a backlog of applicants for future franchisees. Franchise applications were coming in from all over China, with several applicants so sure of the product and the brand they had already placed deposits on their locations prior to signing any deals with us. With the potential new franchisees and our tight overhead budget control, we projected to reach overall profitability at the end of 2011. Joe and I were pretty proud of ourselves for bringing the brand this far, considering that the store sales were much lower than our initial expectations.

In addition, we had opened up a partner store with Megabox movie theatres at a popular Beijing area called Sanlitun. The partnership was working out so well that it had attracted the attention of several large movie chains. After Auntie Anne's opened in Megabox, we learned that our products were so complementary to their snack bar (popcorn, hot dogs, sodas, candies, etc.) that the sales from their snack bar did not drop at all. Instead, our revenue was a complete add-on, but it also provided their guests with a unique snack not offered by competitors. The theatre staffed the store with their employees and they paid for all of the utilities, so we only provided raw ingredients. We only needed to pay for the build-out of the store, which was not that expensive. In exchange, we shared the sales. The arrangement was nearly risk-free for us.

During this time period, the movie industry in China was on an explosive growth path, with each production or distribution company wanting to build their own theatres. Many Hollywood studios would only partner with a Chinese production or distribution firm if it could guarantee that the Hollywood films would be shown on a certain number of screens. As a result, almost every major entertainment production and distribution firm was out there trying to build or acquire theatres. We were contacted by several theatre chains offering the same type of financial arrangements as our partnership with Megabox. These players were planning on opening upwards of fifteen theatres across all parts of China in the next two years, with each theatre featuring Auntie Anne's as the main source of snacks.

Leading up to this time, several events also happened that would alter our fate in China significantly. The first event was the global financial crisis. Our intentions for our first pilot fund were to see if we could create a profitable business in China that could be replicated. Then, we would go out and raise another fund to grow the brand. The crisis changed all of that. Many high-net-worth investors were hurt by the financial crisis and became much more conservative with their investments. Raising new funds would be difficult.

The next problem also related to finances. In 2009 and 2010, institutional funds invested heavily in the food and beverage sector in China, but by 2011, they realized that the performance in this sector was not as high as expected. So, institutional funds slowed or stopped investments in food and beverage brands, especially brands like Auntie Anne's that were capital intensive, yet unproven to be a homerun success. The funds' favorite food categories were rice-based or hot pot-based foods that were already part of the daily living habits of the local Chinese. After a year of talking to potential investors, we were not able to obtain a subsequent round of funding.

Without funding, our backup option was to leverage what little remained of our pilot fund and maximize returns by selling franchises for the rest of the cities and regions in China. This method would be capital efficient, though difficult to manage. In early 2010, Auntie Anne's was still a firm owned by a family member of the original founder. The operations were managed as a family owned organization, which meant that they were not as focused on bottom line returns as public or larger professionally-operated firms were. All that changed when Auntie Anne's was sold to a private equity portfolio firm called FOCUS Brands. FOCUS Brands owned many brands: Carvel, Cinnabon, Moe's Southwest Grill, Schlotzsky's, and the international portion of Seattle's Best Coffee. The private equity group Roake Capital that owned FOCUS Brands also owned Arby's and Cornerstone Bakery. The family-like culture of Auntie Anne's evolved under its ownership. The expectations of us as franchisees became more stringent, though I believed was for the good of the overall brand.

As the master franchisee, we had obligations to open a certain number of stores each year to keep up with the development schedule in our contracts. Unfortunately, we did not keep up with that schedule. Our discussions with FOCUS Brands were all constructive, and they hoped that we could focus on fully developing the Beijing market before trying to spread ourselves thin by franchising countrywide. We did not have a comprehensive support system in place yet, so they were afraid that quality would diminish with each new franchisee.

Our plans to sustain our operations through franchising ended. The growth through partnerships with movie theatres would be good, but difficult without more funding.

In mid-2011, my wife and I also had our first baby, a beautiful daughter. Joe and his wife had also been planning to start a family, but had put off the plans due to the instability of the business. Never did I see myself as someone whose priorities would change so much, so fast. Joe and I had been on a singular mission for the past four years, dedicating and focusing 100 percent of our lives and those of our families on making this brand work in China. We gave the brand our sweat, blood, and tears, literally. Joe and I had been both been hospitalized for various illnesses from stress and from the side effects of living in China, such as the air pollution in my case. Yet, after Karen and I had our daughter, the struggle with the business seemed trivial and less important.

For the first time in four years, I took a step back to examine everything as a whole. Auntie Anne's was going to remain unstable unless we had ample funding. And we did not.

The decision was painful yet simple. We had to walk away.

Shutting Down a
Firm in China

Like everything else we faced in China, this process was not simple. The main issue was that Joe's name was listed as the legal representative for the Chinese entity, which meant that he bore all the risks associated with the firm. Further, shutting down a firm in China was a complicated ordeal that could take up to a year to do so properly. The majority of the firms in China that shut down simply went defunct and left. Owners took their money out of the corporate accounts and that was that. If creditors went after the owners, the government would usually only put a travel restriction on the legal representative, meaning that the legal representative could be apprehended when crossing China's borders.

"He actually went to jail!" Joe and I asked at the same time when our lawyer recounted one such recent example.

"He was detained when he was leaving the country. I was his lawyer and tried calling multiple times on his behalf, but the authorities did not give me any information. That was three months ago," our lawyer explained. His client was Korean and a legal representative for a foreign firm that owed a small sum of money to a supplier.

Our lawyer suggested that this client change the business' legal representative to a local Chinese from another province, one who would be willing to bear the risks for some uncollected debt from creditors. The client agreed, but decided to take a short trip back to Seoul before completing the paperwork. Big mistake. The supplier reported the owed sum to the Beijing Municipal Government, who simply tagged the client's passport in the system. When the client tried to leave Beijing, he was arrested and detained at an unknown location.

"What happened then?" I asked. Joe became quiet and his skin looked a shade paler than it had a few seconds ago.

"The Korean Embassy tried unsuccessfully to visit the client on several attempts and was finally able to see the client to ensure that he was alive and in good condition," he said. In the end, our lawyer had no clue what happened to his client, just that he lost touch.

For most local Chinese, having their passports tagged was not an issue unless they planned on traveling internationally. Foreigners like us, on the other hand, had to leave periodically for visa purposes. Our employee issues at the Labor Bureau were still going on at this time, so our firm might still have to pay out damages to the employees. While we had funds in the account to cover these damages, our goal was to retain as much of the investment to return to our investors. If the employees knew we were shutting down the firm, they would do whatever necessary to ensure that they received their payout immediately.

Our top priority became figuring out how to untangle Joe's name from this mess. We explored the legal way of shutting down the firm, but it was expensive and time-consuming, and still left Joe vulnerable to unknown risks during the process. There were dozens of firms that helped foreigners open up a business in China, but we did not find anyone who knew how to shut down a firm properly. Doing so required the expertise of accountants and lawyers together, and no firm specialized in both.

Similar to what we did when registering the firm, we decided to explore "local" methods of shutting down.

"Just walk away and leave the firm," our lawyer suggested. In fact, that was the most common way a company was shut down in China. Regulations were now in place that stipulated that a firm with no activity for three years would automatically be removed from the system.

"I will help you find a replacement legal representative from my hometown," he continued. "There will be a cost involved, but it will untangle you from all of this mess."

The lawyer mentioned that after the legal representative was changed, we would withdraw all cash from the accounts. We also would not need to pay any damages to employees since we would not be legally associated with the firm any longer. The Beijing Labor Bureau would not chase down a legal representative from another province, since the cost of doing so would be high. However, if we did choose this route, we needed to make sure that we moved our families from our current apartments before the final Labor Bureau judgment came down. The employees would be furious and could resort to violence.

If it was difficult to talk to a spouse about a struggling business and finances, try telling them that the struggling business put the family in harm's way. My baby daughter was at risk. Though it was months after our face-to-face encounter with the employees, Joe and I spent a few days again looking at new apartments and making getaway plans in case the closure of the firm did not go as planned.

After weeks of deliberation, we mapped out a schedule whereby we would close down the stores and be generous with the employees' severance packages.

As for changing the legal representative, the solution sounded great. But we had become paranoid over the years. We always felt that everyone was out to cheat us, so our guard was up constantly. It was tiring. And sad. This lawyer had been our friend and lawyer for the past few years, yet my first thought was how much he was getting for finding the replacement legal representative. In the end though, we were willing to pay any amount to unwind ourselves from this situation safely.

We decided to hire the lawyer's local Chinese friend to replace Joe as the legal representative. As for the case in the Labor Bureau, the lawyer said that we were guaranteed to lose. However, we could hire a trial lawyer to appeal and re-appeal, which could drag out the cases for nearly a year. During that time, the stores would already be shut down, the legal representative changed, and our families moved to new homes. Depending on how much cash remained, we could then decide if we wanted to pay off the employees for lawsuits we considered frivolous.

The Chess Game

Employee's move: Zhu Boxing led the group, and his first move was to incapacitate Joe and me. He approached government bureaus, from health to commercial, to report us for infractions. Previously, when the stores received calls from bureaus, Zhu Boxing would be the person to handle the issues. Now, miraculously, the bureaus had the personal mobile numbers for both Joe and me. Each call from the bureaus became more threatening and demanded that we personally go visit the bureaus. Each visit would suck up one full day of our time, not including the emotional and mental toll that each call took. This strategy was brilliant, since we were so busy that we were unable to deal with the employees.

We had decided to close down the brand and started to work with property management to determine the closing date. In the meantime, our relationship with our store level employees became a real live game of chess; awkward did not begin to explain the situation. On one hand, our most trusted employees and managers were openly rebelling by unionizing against us at the Labor bureau. On the other hand, they remained our employees, whom we could not fire without major repercussions. We wanted to fire them and suffer the consequences, but then

225

that would leave every single one of our stores without management. We needed the employees to hang on for a few more months.

Our move: Since Zhu Boxing was an area manager, he had the freedom to set his schedules and work location. So we began requiring him to work from 9 a.m. to 5 p.m., Monday through Friday. These were also the business hours of the different government bureaus. If he wanted to report us personally, he would have to skip work without approval. He also could not call them because there was usually paperwork to fill out when reporting an employer for anything.

Employees' move: The managers started to show up late to work or completely slack off during work, which made the lower level employees do the same. We checked their attendance in the store using a customary punch clock. This system, however, was easily beatable by having another employee clock in or out for them. Another way to beat it was to simply change the date and the time on the punch clock, allowing the employee to punch their time card for an entire week. Fingerprint-based biometrics punch clocks became available by 2011, but our logistics manager told me that the fingerprint system was just as easy to beat. At this time, we also suspected the employees of stealing sales from the registers, but we could not prove it.

Our move: We installed advanced video cameras that we could control from our laptops. We could move the camera remotely, so we started to monitor the employees continuously. We made our presence shown on purpose by rotating the video camera to follow them when they walked to a different part of the store, and by calling them when we saw areas of improvement. I hated acting like Big Brother, but felt that we had no other recourse at the time.

Employees' move: One of the managers called the video camera's supplier and tried to get the password to the camera, explaining that as manager, it was his duty to watch over the stores. When that angle proved unsuccessful, they simply figured out how to "break" the camera.

The employees would unplug either the video camera itself or the wireless router (both power and network cable) we needed to view the store remotely. Each time we sent a technician to fix the issue, the power or network cable would be pulled again by an employee. However, we were able to catch instances where the managers had shown up consistently late for work, yet their signed punch-in cards showed that they showed up on time.

Our move: We took the videos and punch cards to our lawyer to see if we had enough evidence to fire the managers we caught without the fear of losing a lawsuit at the labor bureau. Unfortunately, the strategy did not work. According to our lawyer, since we as employers had access to change the date and time of the videos, the system we used to catch them skipping work was not valid. We needed real proof, like a signed confession or recorded voice confession. Otherwise, we had a good chance of losing a lawsuit for wrongful termination. My fault for thinking that video evidence was good enough.

Our move: In the final weeks of operations, we wanted to separate ourselves from the brand, as the employees still had the habit of showing up at our apartments randomly. So, when we finally informed the employees that we were shutting down, we said we had been "fired" by the firm and had no more responsibilities at Auntie Anne's in China. For all future communication, we told them, please go through our lawyer, as he was the designated person to act on the firm's behalf.

Employees' move: Our first accountant established a financial process by which the sales from the stores were deposited first into my personal bank account. The accountants then transferred the funds into the company account after paying for things requiring cash, as it was difficult to withdraw cash from the company account. The employees informed us that since Joe and I had been fired by the company, they could no longer deposit the money into a personal account. In addition, they would not send staff schedules and sales reports to us anymore, as we were not responsible. Essentially, the employees cut us out of all operations.

Our move: Since we controlled the company chops, we wrote official letters from the company for anything we needed. We sent a notice for the employees to deposit all sales directly into the company account. The notice was delivered by our accountant with a warning that if the employees defied it, they would be reported to the police for theft of funds. Management of the day-to-day activities was routed through our accountants and lawyers, but we still requested the employees to send all relevant reports to us.

Employee's move: Managers from each store started to send in time schedules late so they could not get preapproved. The hours on the schedules were also extremely inflated, showing that all employees had worked eighty hours per week. Overtime pay was 1.5 times normal pay, so the overall sum was not insignificant.

Our move: Working with the lawyer, we informed the managers that no unapproved overtime would be paid. Every store had ample employees to staff it without anyone having to work overtime. The lawyer then became much tougher in tone and told the employees to take the case to the Labor Bureau. Should they do that, they would not get paid until the conclusion of the case, which could be over a year away. In addition, we would review the videotapes and threatened to countersue them for lying, even though we knew we probably would not win.

Our final move: The bickering and plotting had become childish. We took a step back and evaluated the entire situation, then threw in the towel on our battle against the employees. Despite the employee disputes, we did not overlook the fact that closing down the stores would adversely affect the lives of everyone. We felt horrible about deciding to close down and about how it would affect our investors, our employees, and our trusted suppliers. Joe and I informed each of our employees personally of the plans. Several employees who had dedicated themselves wholly to the concept broke down and cried. We cried along with them. They had the same hopes and dreams as we did.

In the end, we decided to pay out a generous severance package to all employees, even the ones who were suing us. Many of the employees had sacrificed and worked so hard through the years that we wanted to take care of them. We had not been able to make the brand a success and it was our fault entirely.

For several employees who were in financial distress, Joe and I even shelled out money from our own pockets to help them out with monthly expenses. Through our contacts, we also placed certain employees at other firms to ensure that they did not feel any pains of unemployment. However, we did not feel any outrageous demands were justified for the employees who were suing us. We also did not want additional trouble (like fearing for our safety) if we followed our lawyer's advice and walked away without paying.

We were able to hand over our registration for the foreign entity to another chain that wanted to enter China. They assumed all liabilities for our China entities. What I heard after we did this was that the new owners offered the employees a sum less than half of what they demanded. They had their lawyer discuss the situation with the judge presiding over the case. The new owner's position was that if it was going to cost any more, they would walk away from the firm and the employees would receive nothing. The judge personally called each of the employees and encouraged them to take the settlement. The lawsuits were then settled out of court.

Epilogue
The Final Drip

Living in a new culture could change a person—in my case, it gave me a temper where I had not had one before. Initially, I lashed out at the inefficiencies, the differences in attitude. I screamed at waiters and cab drivers. I pushed to the front of lines, shoving aside old people and toddlers in the process. I stopped thanking people for anything. I learned to clear my throat by filling streets and walls with my loogies. I hated who I was becoming.

For a while, I blamed China for everything I despised. Only when I saw other expats who were further along in this self-destructive process did I realize that I was on the same path. They were constantly complaining about things they could not change, things that made Beijing unique and special. "Bad attitude" did not begin to explain their outlook towards China, and their negativity served as a reminder of who I did not want to become. I had chosen to live here, and the culture was not going to change for me or any other expat.

To survive in peace, I learned to accept and respect the differences between living in Beijing and living in the US. Today, I had come to cherish them, though living here was still challenging in some respects. The chatty taxi drivers were once annoying, but now I enjoyed their conversations. Every restaurant serves hot water in Beijing, in the winter or summer, as it does not shock the body like ice water does. Once an avid drinker of only ice water, I now ask for hot water even when I visited the US. The selection in Beijing for many types of cuisine was better than any other city I visited, from hole-in-the-wall cafes to fancy restaurants. If I wanted to eat Italian food, I could easily think of ten places that served great Italian food within twenty minutes of my apartment. This was a luxury that I have not found in San Francisco or in the DC area. I once considered the street food here crap compared to that in Bangkok or Taipei, but now I crave the crunchy, savory crêpes served outside of clubs, and the grilled lamb kebabs that filled the night with the fragrant barbeque smoke. The pollution was horrible throughout, but I have learned to monitor the Air Quality Index before deciding how much time to spend outside.

Perhaps the main reason I had come to love Beijing was the people I had met here— international, adventurous, and open-minded. My friends here were all pursuing similar journeys. We were all in search of something exciting, something different. Though we may have been pursuing different industries—art, academics, a pretzel franchise—the journeys we took to living here strengthened our bond quickly. I found that I developed more close friends in the last four years than in any other period of my life. For that, I am grateful.

Regarding Auntie Anne's, we shut down our self-operated stores in the fourth quarter of 2011 and the partnership stores in 2012.

"Bittersweet" was the best word to describe how I felt. The relief I experienced was indescribable, as if I had been released from jail. Yet it was hard to let go, as we had poured so much of ourselves into this project. We now understood intimately the enormous challenges of opening a startup business, and gained tremendous respect for all those who had taken this path.

For the first time in years, I had restful sleep. Joe and I both took a short break to regain our strength and to ponder our next moves. Despite our experiences, I enjoyed the food industry. My gut kept telling me that I am far from done in this industry and in this region.

The international group of FOCUS Brands was led by seasoned leaders who share my dream to build brands. I love their vision to be "Legendary Brand Builders" and respect their experience. They offered me the opportunity to join FOCUS Brands International and I jumped at the chance to continue on this journey.

Even today when I reflect on what we experienced in China, the issues were non-stop. Through the years, I was more scared of the quiet periods, since these were a signal that something was about to smack us in the face. Random inspections. Labor problems. Supplier issues. Like drops of water hitting my forehead. The only constant was the inevitability of the next unexpected crisis, the next China Twist.

Appendices

The Real Deal
Disclosure

The following section is not meant to serve as legal advice, and anyone seeking to do business in China should have their own advisors and counsel. Please note that I am not a lawyer; all information from this book (including the appendices section) is NOT a substitute for legal advice. The readers should seek legal counsel before moving forward.

Appendix A

Firm Registration/ Corporation Structure

Many of the regulations have changed over the past few years, and as they are constantly updated, any information we provide here may already be dated. However, if we had the opportunity to register everything again starting in 2011, this is how I would do it for Auntie Anne's.

Off-Shore Entity

Figuring out how to setup our corporate structure was not an easy task. It took a lot of planning, and discussions with different lawyers, for us to put together a structure that worked. Everyone talked about a Cayman Islands or British Virgin Islands (BVI) entity for tax-saving purposes, but setting this structure up required lawyers who were familiar with the laws there. Doing this was not as easy as it sounded, especially considering our small budget.

There were several layers to consider when setting up our firm. First, the core partnership involved Joe, Jonathan, Justin, and I. Since Joe and I were the main operating figures, we had a different return structure than Jonathan and Justin. For our partnership, we set up a limited liability corporation in Delaware under the name China Franchise Group (CFG), LLC. The set-up process required online registration to get a business ID, which we used to establish our corporate bank accounts. Joe and I had to implement a separate management contract to reflect our return structure. The CFG account was the one in which the four partners invested funds.

For the investors, we explored Cayman, BVI, and Hong Kong (HK). Registration in the Cayman Islands was preferred by many hedge funds, since it has very lenient laws to protect the investors, ability for its firms to be listed on the HK stock exchange, and exemption clauses for closely-held funds. BVI has much lower registration costs, no offering documentation requirements, no capital registration requirements, and no audit requirements. Both BVI and Cayman have no taxation, which is one of the top reasons why so many firms register there. Hong Kong has a sound legal system, no foreign exchange controls, and low business taxes.

All three were based on the English Common Law, but the Cayman and BVI seemed very foreign to us at the time, as we had no friends familiar with the registration process there. All three locations were good to use if one wanted to build a shell company based on simple templates, but our return structures were not easy to implement. Our return structure was based on performance, and each dollar invested into the venture became its pro rata equity from day one. We learned that the return structure we wanted was very difficult to draft in legal documents. If one were a hedge fund, the legal fees would be only a small percentage of the overall fund value. In our case, it was a much different matter. In the end, we decided on HK due to its proximity to China and ease of setting up Chinese firms from there.

The investor documentation was going to be difficult regardless of where we incorporated. Faiz (who was acting as a lawyer for us) agreed to spend the dozens of hours necessary to help us draft the investor documentation.

Investors would receive a confidential offering memorandum (Subscription Agreement), which laid out the share structure and other basic legal terms. Investors would ultimately sign the Subscription Agreement, which would be governed under the laws of Hong Kong. Investor funds would be invested into our HK entity, Pretzels China Limited. CFG would also be an investor of the HK entity.

Once all the investment dollars were invested into the HK entity, that entity would invest the money into a Chinese entity. The entity in China would be a Wholly Foreign-Owned Entity (WFOE), which would be 100 percent owned by Pretzels China Limited. In China, the type of shareholder determines what type of entity it becomes. If some of the shareholders were Chinese and some foreign, it would be a joint venture. The simplest type of corporation to set up in China is a local entity, but that requires that all shareholders be Chinese citizens.

Although this was not officially stated anywhere, the local firms were not scrutinized like the foreign entities and generally had a much easier time obtaining licensing and other approvals. Often, foreigners with experience in China find local friends or significant others to act as their shareholders. They have side contracts to protect themselves, though these side agreements were difficult to enforce. The issue there would shift to trusting the local partner to act in accordance to the original agreement, since control of the firm would be under the partner's control.

Chops: What they are and why they matter

Before we begin, let me explain the concept of a "chop" and its importance in China. Whereas signatures are important in the US and elsewhere in the Western world in approving decisions by an individual or a firm, a signature is useless in China; it is too easy to forge. Instead, China uses a "chop," which is a carved seal that is pressed into red ink to stamp a document. They used to be made out of stone, but now they are made out of rubber and plastic. The seal itself and the chop maker must be approved by the Public Safety Bureau (PSB), and supposedly it is very difficult to create identical chops. Banks and government agencies have electronic chop scanners to detect the authenticity of the chop.

Each company is issued several types of chops, including a company chop, financial chop, and contract chop. Each legal representative also has a chop for their own signatures. The company chop is by far the most important, as it provides for all legal execution for all of the firm's documents. The financial chop is used for checks, along with the personal chop of the legal representative. The contract chop is usually used for trade contracts, but the company chop can be used for the same purpose as well.

The General Manager (GM) controls the chop in most cases. Since most documents require the chop, who manages the chop is an issue. The chop is needed for virtually everything, but there is no way that a GM of a firm can run from government bureau to government bureau every day to chop documents. Of course, documents could be brought back to the office to be chopped, but doing that is time-consuming and inefficient. Many firms have an elaborate system to control the chop if it must leave the office, using two or more employees from different departments to travel with the chop. If a firm loses control of their chop, they essentially lose control of their firm.

It is of the utmost importance to respect and understand the usage of the chop when doing business in China.

Local versus Wholly Foreign-Owned Entity (WFOE)

If I were to open this firm again, I would explore any opportunities to open up a local firm rather than a WFOE.

What are some of the considerations of a local firm versus those of WFOEs? Capital injection and repatriation is probably the top issue for foreign investors. Since RMB is tightly controlled, each person is only allowed to exchange $50,000 USD per person annually in or out of the RMB. For a firm trying to invest millions into China, this issue presents a problem: how do you get the money in? Once the invested firm is profitable, the question becomes how to get the money out.

Though not condoned, many small firms used a network of friends, who may have personal needs to exchange RMB in or out of USD. One could find enough people to help even for million dollar exchanges. The method is not clean but it works. Going through the WFOE method requires a firm to inject the registered capital into a local bank account, where it is left with low interest and in USD. The WFOE then needs to go through a painful capital verification process with the State Administration of Foreign Exchange (SAFE) to get approval to send and receive the capital in China. Even if a firm had millions in the bank, a WFOE is only allowed to convert at most $50,000 USD into RMB at any given time. The process is arduous and tiring. After spending $50,000 USD, one needs to bring every single receipt to the bank to make copies, get them chopped by various bank personnel, and then wait to get approved by SAFE for the exchange. For us, when we first transferred our capital in 2008 into China, the exchange rate was 7.6 RMB to 1 USD. Through the years that it took us to spend the investment amount, the exchange rate dropped to 6.5 RMB to 1 USD. We lost 15 percent in our registered capital value because of this capital injection process.

Local firms inherently go through a lot fewer inspections and processes. All foreign firms must be approved and registered with the Ministry of Commerce (MOFCOM), the government body that deals with foreign firms. This is in addition to all of the other bureaus like the State Administration of Industry and Commerce (SAIC), the Health Bureau, Environmental Bureau, Fire Safety Bureau, Labor Bureau, Social Security & Insurance Bureau, Customs Bureau, Public Security Bureau (PSB), and Tax Bureaus (there are separate tax bureaus for local and federal taxes). We even had to deal with a Measurements and Scale bureau for our weighing scales. No issues arose with customs when we leveraged a local importing company to import our raw ingredients, but when we used our own company name to import, all of our shipments received "special" treatment. MOFCOM is the only official additional bureau a WFOE has to work with, relative to a local firm. In reality, all bureaus give extra attention to the WFOE. Each random inspection from any bureau is a tax on management's time and efforts. For a small firm, this tax on time is tiring and all-consuming.

How could a foreign investor setup a local firm? To qualify for a local firm, the shareholders must all be Chinese ID holders so that the firm was 100 percent Chinese-owned. For small businesses, this area is where one needs trusted local friends or partners to act in this role. However, larger firms can leverage the Variable Interest Entity (VIE) structure, a series of contracts that allowed foreign investors control over Chinese firms they do not own. The VIE structure has been used by foreign investors as a loophole to invest in certain industries that were banned under Chinese laws from having foreign investors, such as the internet and telecom. Unfortunately, the VIE has not been truly tested in the court system. In the summer of 2011, Yahoo even lost control of their stake in Alipay when Alipay owner Jack Ma transferred the firm to himself without notifying Yahoo. Despite the contracts in place, Yahoo had little to no leverage.

Leveraging a local structure is also inherently risky. Most major corporations would not take this route, but it can be cost-efficient for small enterprises.

Other Considerations for Firm Registration

Every corporation in China needs one person to be the legal responsible person (法人; *faren*). This person ultimately shoulders the liabilities for anything that happens with this firm—or, to put it bluntly, he or she is the one who goes to jail first if the firm is found to be doing anything criminal. The *faren* can be a holder of Chinese ID or even a foreigner. Another important person is the board supervisor (监事; *jianshi*), who oversees any official board actions for the firm. This role theoretically acts as a check and balance to the power that the *faren* has. However, unlike the *faren*, the board supervisor does not have liabilities and risks regarding what happens with the firm.

The *faren* will have a lot of running around to do to get the company set up. He or she controls the company, so his or her personal chop will be required to stamp every government or bank document. The *faren* takes on a lot of responsibilities, and this position should not be entered into lightly because of the risks it poses.

Once the firm selects a *faren* and board secretary, the investor needs to understand what type of firm to register for. We made a mistake by registering for a restaurant firm and not a restaurant *management* firm. A restaurant firm needs to be situated at a location that could be the restaurant. The location required approvals from the Health Bureau, Environmental Bureau, and many other bureaus. For someone who only wants to open one or two restaurants, this method is fine. However, since we wanted to be a franchise with our headquarters situated in an office, this method was not ideal for us.

For the restaurant registration, the business category of future subsidiaries must be covered by the headquarters' business category. An example is that if the future subsidiary wants to sell baked items, that category to sell "baked items" must be part of the headquarters' category even if the headquarter only sold drinks today. This proved to be an issue for us, as it meant that our first location at the Gate Mall had to have a full business category for everything we intended for Auntie Anne's to sell in the future. If we wanted to sell sandwiches at a new location, for example, we would need to go back to update the business category at the Gate. Unfortunately, getting any type of business category approved for the Gate turned out to be very difficult, due to the Gate's small size. A management company could have subsidiaries that are restaurants with different business categories, so it was not hindered by this roadblock. In addition, registering a management company automatically gives you the ability to franchise, whereas a regular restaurant registration does not allow for that. None of our legal counsel or advisers informed us about this simple issue, even though we explained our goals to them about franchising and opening multiple stores.

Another major issue we had was figuring out where we should register the firm, as a firm was based in the district in which the headquarters are located. Beijing has over ten districts, and the leniency of the bureaus differs in each. The most important relationship to have here is with the Tax Bureau, as it has the most impact on earnings. Each bureau wants firms to incorporate in their district, due to the future tax earnings. It is difficult to switch districts after registration, so choose a district wisely and with care. Registering the holding company in a tax-friendly city such as Tianjin or other up-and-coming cities could work well for you, as these cities may have many tax-break incentives to draw in businesses.

Your firm's trademark is one of the first things you should register. Chances are if the firm has international appeal, someone has already registered the name and trademark in China, even if that someone is not a representative of the firm that owns that name and trademark. Trademark squatters are busy in China locking down the names and trademarks of any firms that could potentially enter the country. The actual act of registering a trademark and firm name takes a few hours with a trademark lawyer, and cost less than $1,000 USD. However, the total process of locking down a trademark could take more than a year.

Registering the Business

Once you have decided on the structure and other details about your business, the actual implementation and registration could be handled by a local agent. If you Google "China firm registration," hundreds of firms will show up. Many of these firms could handle the basics of firm registration, though you need to interview them to see how much time they would spend on your case. Some firms are understaffed, so delays will happen due to their inability to show up in time at the bureaus to pick up the paperwork required to push onto the next step. Most firms could walk you through how to fill out forms, but mistakes would still happen due to the ambiguous nature of the forms. Obviously, firms that operate only in English would be two to three times more expensive than firms that only operate in Chinese. If the registration were coordinated through a law firm, the law firm would help fill out the paperwork.

However, they would still farm out visiting the bureaus and registering the business to a local registration firm. Few law firms would waste their own time to wait in the long lines at each bureau.

Before starting the registration process, make sure you figure out what type of business you need so that you register for the correct type. There is nothing worse than going through the entire process only to find out, as we did, that you registered for the wrong type of business and have to start over. To figure out the right business scope, check with a few agents and advisors in case you have had any miscommunication issues.

The actual registration process is laborious and time-consuming. The official published timeline only describes an ideal situation where all paperwork was filled correctly and chopped in the right locations. In most cases, there would be some paperwork that was not filled out properly or chops you did not realize you needed to get. To complicate matters further, many government employees will not explain which parts are wrong, but would reject all the paperwork at once. The onus is on the applicant to figure out where the mistake was, correct it, and resubmit the paperwork. Each small mistake will take at least one day to fix since these bureaus are usually only opened for a few hours each day, and you could spend a few hours waiting in line. For example, we often dealt with forms that were ambiguous in how they asked for certain information. Although we had all of the right information, the bureau members kept rejecting it. In the end, we learned they wanted the information to be filled out in a very specific order. Even our agents were unfamiliar with this order, so the process took many tries to get it right. Of course, while the bureau employees could have taken less than a minute to explain it to us, no one bothered.

Perhaps the most common, yet costliest, method that large corporations follow when entering China is to leverage a law firm in their home country. The foreign law firm will sub-contract out to a reputable

China-based law firm, and this firm would then find the local agents to help process the paperwork. This process was as time-consuming as it was expensive, however, and it was more efficient to directly approach a Chinese law firm or the China office of an international law firm that can provide services in English. If you have partners or contacts in China, approaching a reputable local registration agent directly will be the most cost- and time-efficient thing to do.

Appendix B

Chinese Labor Laws

There are many online resources about the Chinese Labor Contract Law enacted on January 1, 2008 that caused us so much trouble. Here are the lessons we learned from our experiences with that law and the run-ins we had with our employees over it:

Overtime: There are no "salaried" employees in China as there are in the US, which means that all salaries need to be broken down into an hourly wage. Each month, the government determines a set number of hours as regular working hours. Any hours worked over this prescribed range of time are subject to overtime pay at 1.5 times the regular salary. Holiday pay is three times that of regular pay. Many upper-level (i.e. better-paid) white collar employees will not complain about working overtime, so this issue is mostly important when dealing with lower-level white collar employees and blue collar workers.

Many Western firms in China (from software development firms to services firms) assumed that an employee should work hard to finish the work, even if it included overtime. However, if there were documented cases where the employees work overtime (time cards, approved time schedules, etc.), the employees would have a case against their employer for overtime. Further, a firm would often have rules that all overtime must be pre-approved before payment, but would knowingly not approve any overtime. Many of these firm paid dearly when the employees produced proof that they had worked overtime and demanded compensation.

One way to manage this situation is to clearly communicate with employees about expectations for working hours. In our case, we calculated by total monthly hours and reviewed the schedules often to ensure we were not paying out too much in overtime. When the overtime pay reached a certain amount, we hired another full time employee at the store to minimize the costs. For back office employees, we kept track of employees' overtime and give them days off in lieu of paying overtime.

Terms of Employment: Each employer may offer a probationary period to a new employee, but a contract must be in effect even during this time. For any employee who works without an employment contract, the employer is subject to paying the employee double for the entire time that employee was without a contract.

A two-year contract allows for a two-month trial period, and a three-year contract allows for a six-month probationary term. After a contract expires, the employee must be offered another contract or be let go. If no renewal contract is offered and the employee keeps working, the government sees that as the same thing as having that employee work without a contract. After the second contract ends, the employer must offer either a lifetime (yes, *lifetime*) contract or let the employee go. An employer needs to ensure that the employee is worth the lifetime contract. Though we never faced the situation, I have heard of people making the employees "officially" quit and then resign the contract to avoid the lifetime contract. This approach is definitely unfair for the employees and could trigger significant internal pushback should employees stick together to fight the practice.

Social insurances: Even during the probationary period, the employer should provide all social benefits and insurances for all employees. There are six social insurances (medical, pension, unemployment, occupational injury, maternity, and housing fund) that Chinese law requires all employees to receive (note that all employees, even men, receive maternity insurance). For lower wage employees, these six insurances could represent an additional 40 percent or more of their monthly pay that the employers need to pay.

Foreign investors often mistakenly use only the employee wages, and not their total compensation, to calculate labor costs. As a result, many firms do whatever they could to avoid paying these insurances. In reality, most small-sized employers do not provide all the insurances, only a few that their employees desire. In many firms, for example, employees want more cash instead of these social insurances. Some firms also think that it was sufficient to have the employee sign a waiver forgoing insurance, but this practice is not legal.

The insurances have a huge impact on the employers' bottom line; thus, the playing field is not even for a local competitor that pays almost no social insurances, compared to a foreign firm that pays for everything. More and more firms have been paying the full insurances, however, as the employees have become more knowledgeable about their rights.

Termination of employees: Perhaps the touchiest subject of all is how to terminate an employee. The best way to do so is by not renewing the contract when it ends. Employers who want to fire an employee as soon as possible should document as much as possible. Document any issues that the employee has had, review the document with the employee, and make the employee sign it. Terminating an employee without cause is illegal, and the employer is subject to paying out a three-month penalty in addition to the employee's severance (based on the amount of time he or she worked at the firm).

Cause is difficult to prove without hard evidence. A friend of mine had an accountant who was so upset that she was being terminated that she slapped the employer as hard as she could in front of his employees and customers. She then proceeded to vandalize the surrounding tables until another employee restrained her and removed her. Even though my friend had a police report about the incident, the accountant sued him for unlawful termination. Somehow she got to the employees who witnessed the scene, and none of them would corroborate my friend's story. The incident also happened in a location where video cameras could not record. As a result, this is now a case of his word versus hers; most likely, he would lose and have to pay for wrongful termination.

An employer should take care and plan ahead when terminating an employee. The employee would undergo difficult times as s/he looks for the next opportunity, and the employer needs to be sensitive to this hard period. Nonetheless, the employer needs to establish (through signed documentation or other hard evidence) a clear, indisputable reason to terminate before doing so. All it takes is one upset employee to start a union against the whole firm.

Sign-off agreement (when starting): When an employee joins the firm, s/he needs to be given an employee manual and handbook. There needs to be a sign-off document to prove that the employee received the handbook, or nothing in the manual is applicable to the employee.

Appendix c

Franchise Laws

History shows that the concept of a franchise—the desire to expand, the lack of expansion capital and the need to overcome distance—has been the integral growth engines of governments and churches. The earliest record of a chain store franchisee originated—wait for it—in China around 200 B.C.E. when a businessman named Lo Kass operated several retail units using the franchisee/franchisor arrangement[4]. Thus, it is no surprise that there are more franchises offered in China than most other countries. Unofficially, China is reported to have over 4,000 franchise systems, versus 3,000 or so in the US.

The concept of franchising is second-nature to Chinese people, though headlines in China are dominated by major US franchises like McDonald's and KFC. The evolution of franchise operations in China is far different than that of US operations. In the US, even as early as 1979, the government required the disclosure of business information related to the franchise on the franchising opportunities[5]. Today, the Uniform Franchise Offering Circular (UFOC) is a standard, detailed disclosure in the US that every franchisor must make before any funds are transferred between it and franchisees.

In China, however, ambiguous laws appeared in 2005. Though it has been revised several times, most people still find the laws extremely ambiguous. For example, according to the franchise regulations enacted in 2007, franchisors only need to have been in business for one year and have

---

4   Franchising - The How To Book, Lloyd Tarbutton

5   Federal Trade Commission Rule of 1979

two operating stores. However, the laws do not say where the operating stores need to be, nor how this rule is enforced. Supposedly, there are other disclosure laws as well. The franchisor needs to provide the following information thirty days prior to signing a franchise agreement: the franchisor's name, domicile, amount of registered capital, business category, intellectual property (IP) rights, and involvement in lawsuits. From our experience, the franchisor needs to have a "franchising" business category on the business license of the Chinese entity that will be selling the franchise. For any firms that are registered as a management company, the business category is included automatically. Again, there are no enforcement agencies and few precedent-setting lawsuits, so these ambiguous laws are still subject to interpretation, usually by individual agents.

As a result of these loosely-enforced government rules, franchising has taken on a different look and feel in China. While the use of lawsuits to enforce a contract is on the rise, the control of the franchisees is often based on control of supplies or raw ingredients that the franchisor can measure.

Although we had many requests for franchisees from the very beginning, we realized several key differences between how franchises worked in China and how they worked in the US. First, there was a handful or more of fraudulent franchises in the 4,000 franchises that exist in China. For example, I knew someone who was starting a barbeque franchise out of Beijing at the same time we were opening up our Auntie Anne's. In less than a year's time, this person had grown to twenty franchises all over China, but their foundation was based on made-up traditions and "successes" backed up by claims on their website and numerous blog posts made by one person under assumed names. Although their few directly-owned stores all bankrupted in months, they were able to continue selling the franchises. Despite franchise laws prohibiting the sale of franchises unless the firm had at least two operating stores for more than a year, this firm was selling actively with no stores at all. Obviously, local Chinese were wary—and weary—of these local, unknown franchisers.

Second, we realized that the financial structures of the franchises here were different from those we were accustomed to. While US-based franchises charged an initial franchise fee, much of the profit comes at the royalty percentage that they took from all sales and the markup on the raw ingredients. Well, enforcement is a major issue in China, so smaller franchisees that could not monitor the franchisees day-to-day would rely on initial franchise fees to make their money. On a small scale, why take $10 over ten years if they could get $5 today? Some will charge an annual flat-rate franchise fee for the use of the brand. If the products sold were very distinct, they could also charge a markup for the raw ingredients.

The fact that the most successful food and beverage brands in China invest in and operate their own stores says a lot about the state of franchising in China. Like anywhere, it is difficult to find partners and franchisees who would care as much about the quality and consistency of a product as the brand owner does. Until the franchisor has a foolproof methodology to launch and manage the quality of its stores, sustained expansion will be difficult to achieve.

In 2011, McDonald's started to grant franchises selectively in non-strategic cities, but it had taken them decades to smooth out the operations and internal controls. Even then, they sold existing stores to franchisees so that the entire system was operating smoothly first. Then, they had all of the controls in place across every aspect of the business. I know of many cases where business concepts that started as franchises later reacquired the franchises they created so that they could directly manage the brand.

Having said this, there are ways for franchises to be successful in China, even in the food business. Subway is a good example. They now have over a decade of experience in China, but they had to grow their market from scratch. Most people in China were not used to eating cold meat and uncooked vegetables before Subway arrived, and to spread it over another uncommon item, the bread roll, with unfamiliar sauces made the overall sale difficult. But Subway stuck to their guns and provided the same type of sandwiches with ever-improving quality and control systems. The first wave of franchisees may not have done well, but they laid the foundation for the current owners to prosper. In major cities where there are many foreigners, Subway has grown rapidly and has been able to penetrate the local market.

The following are some more key lessons we learned in our franchise experience:

Strict adherence to the rules: Although a franchisor/franchisee relationship should not be based on policing every rule, a precedent needs to be set early on that transgressions would not be tolerated. We were too accommodating with Locksley, and he stepped all over us. We should have applied penalties for transgressions and been willing to go to extremes (like stopping shipment of raw ingredients and taking legal action to enforce our rules) to show that while we wanted to work together, the rules still needed to be followed.

Putting skin in the game: In the traditional franchise, the franchisor puts up the brand, ingredients, or know-how, but does not risk anything. Whether this was an investment into a joint venture (JV) with the franchisee or commitment in terms of increased support, the franchisee/partner would be more inclined to put forth effort and investment if the franchisor could show commitment. For example, Costa Coffee, from the U.K., entered China on a JV with a large local firm named Hualian (BHG). Costa brought the brand and know-how while BHG brought the local management and connections. While they definitely had a period of adjustment in terms of working together, Costa Coffee has grown quickly and successfully through China in the past few years.

Supplier management: As a franchisor, you need to make sure that the raw ingredients are approved, and ensure that they came from reputable suppliers. Make the effort to identify *all* of the franchisee's suppliers, right down to the napkins and cleaning supplies. Periodically audit the suppliers, since it is easy for the franchisee to switch to cheaper options without notice. The best scenario is that you manage all suppliers centrally so that no one takes shortcuts, but that requires enough presence in a certain region to make the effort worthwhile.

Dedication to training: You need to make a significant investment to develop initial and continuous training for the franchisees, from product preparation to service management. The plan and schedule to provide training is easily set, but hard to implement. We needed a dedicated team to train new employees and franchisees. There were also times when we wanted to send trainers to the franchisees, but they ignored our requests because our agreement stipulated that they needed to pay for travel costs. Their refusal to make this small investment prevented regular training due to the initial financial arrangement. Ultimately, training is an investment you cannot overlook.

Support team: Each franchisee should have a representative responsible for supporting the franchisee, someone who is constantly in communication with the franchisee to understand their issues and the lessons they learn along the way. This person acts both as an enforcer of brand image and quality, as well as a true consultant to help the business improve. This support person would also work with the franchisee to provide customized marketing advice.

Appendix D

Importing Regulations

The importing process was perhaps our greatest challenge. Each shipment could have an unknown result, despite the fact that we were shipping the same products. Rules and regulations change often, based on the dynamic relationship between China and the US. Since the process is slightly different depending on what one is shipping (food items, equipment, etc.), this section will focus more on food-related items.

Here is the general break-down of the overall process.

1. **Understanding the parties involved:** There are many parties involved when importing, including:

   a) Producer: Party from whom one purchases the products. This party is responsible for providing most of the original documentation.

   b) Freight forwarder: The logistics firm that assists with shipping the products from point A to point B. These firms can cover the full gamut of services, from pure logistics services (those that have no involvement with the paperwork) to full service providers (e.g. DHL or FedEx).

   c) Importer: The firm that holds the importing license. For franchising firms that do not have importing license, a 3rd party firm with an importing license is required to help bring in the products. These importing agents can usually walk through all of the details about the required documentation and can outline the process. Most importers only know the details about a few product categories, so you may need to use several agents to properly import if there are many Stock Keeping Units (SKUs).

d) **Distributor:** If the product is for end user retail consumption, the distributor's information is required to import.

e) **Customs Reporting Officer:** A person either on the importing firm's staff or an outsourced person who has a license to report products to customs.

f) **Storage provider:** When the products arrive, they can go into a bonded warehouse where one chooses not to pay taxes on the products until one takes them out. Import taxes need to be paid in full before any products can leave the bonded warehouse. There are also cold storage bonded warehouses available in certain ports for items that need refrigeration, but the cost of storage here can be high. The type of warehouse you should use depends on what your products will be used for.

2. **Documentation:** Prepare all documentation from the producer for the product. For food products used by the importer and not sold retail, the documentation includes the Certification of Origin and Certificate of Protocol/Analysis. The original documents need to be issued or approved by "official authorities," as the documentation that comes directly from the production firms is not accepted. There needs to be an official-looking chop or stamp on the documentation or else officials will not approve it.

For retail products, the products need to be properly labeled in Chinese, including nutrition information and information about the distributor. It is best to have the labels reviewed by the importing firm and the customs agent before shipping.

However, labels can be applied in the bonded warehouses, as these warehouses are officially still in "international" territory. You need to figure out how difficult this process is, and it depends on the port of entry and the relationship the importing agent has with the officers.

3. **Understanding the tax code:** Tax code changes, and understanding which tax code fits which product is tricky. We encountered a classic example of this when we imported a blended flour mix, for which no direct classification existed. The agent will try to minimize taxes by reporting what they think they can get away with, though issues could arise with that method. For example, we were classified under a proprietary blend where the tax rate is around 25 percent, but then after three years, customs agents opened up our shipment and tested it. They discovered the blend to be mostly flour, which has a 65 percent duty (and then another 17 percent added tax on the combined value of the product and duty).

Customs claimed we had misled them about our blended mix and wanted to back charge us for all of the previous shipments. Instantly, we had a full shipment trapped in a bonded warehouse and past liabilities on all our previous shipments. We negotiated and reduced the 65 percent to something a little less, but we had to pay it all before customs would release our shipment. Many of the food products have specific definitions in fine print on the tax code, so the importing agent needs to be detailed. For example, the tax on alcohol depends on the alcohol content, not the category of alcohol.

Many of the protected products (such as rice and flour) have special quotas and limitations imposed by the government, so importing them required additional applications to fall within the quota. However, for certain products, only state-owned companies have the allocations for these quotas, giving them an oligopoly.

After you have paid the taxes, the products can be shipped out of the bonded warehouses and into the importer's warehouse. However, food products technically cannot be used until they get the approval of the CIQ.

4. **China Inspection & Quarantine (CIQ):** Once the products arrive and pass customs (meaning that taxes have been paid), the products need to be tested by the CIQ. However, sometimes testing can be completed before the actual shipment. To find out if this can be done, one needs to check with the importing agent about the sample requirements and process. Once CIQ officially passes the samples, the importer will receive a chopped document that officially allows the proper usage or retail sales for the product.

    In conclusion, the importing strategy for each firm needs to be customized. The port of entry, the nature of the goods, and the relationships with the Customs and CIQ officers all play a part in how the strategy is implemented. For example, for firms that intend to distribute nationwide, most importing firms recommend importing through Shenzhen, where the implementation of these rules is more lax. Though importing laws and processes are supposed to be the same throughout China, they are nonetheless applied differently from region to region and from person to person.

Appendix E

Internships

Over the years, many people have asked us for details on how we operated our internship program. Here are some lessons we learned:

Establishing the program

- Understand the type of tasks you want the interns to perform (clerical, research, analysis, design, etc). In our case, we looked for interns of all types to help us make our tasks more efficient. The general rule of thumb I used was that the intern needed to help me save time. I did not mind spending time on one-on-one training, but the time spent could not be more than the total time I would have spent if I had completed the intern's tasks myself.
- Develop framework around the program and tasks (pay/reimbursement structure, working hours, expectations, management structure, capacity to host the intern, etc.).
- Present the internship program in a professional, concise manner.
- Post/advertise in appropriate locations. In my experience, posting directly with universities has been the most effective. If possible, set up formal relationships with one or two universities so that administrators or counselors can refer the best students.

Application/interview process:

- If you put a lot of work into planning the internship program, students will be attracted by the effort. Making the process competitive (but not overly so) will attract attention as well, as something which is difficult to obtain often attracts a desirable candidate.

- For me, the most important aspects of the interview were to see if we had the right opportunity for the candidate and if the candidate had a good attitude and the ability to learn and work hard. If those two criteria matched, I hired, even if the person was not the most qualified.

Running an internship program:

- Understand the goals of the interns and match projects to the interns based on those goals. If there are tedious or boring tasks, mix them in with exciting ones.
- Provide feedback promptly. Interns are often inexperienced, so feedback could be nothing more than an affirmation of the direction in which they are heading. If they are on the wrong track, it is better to catch any mistakes early. The lazy interns will not ask for feedback too much, and they will fade out naturally, meaning that they ultimately would not waste your time.

Miscellaneous:

- Assign a few interns to an important project in the event that any one intern cannot deliver as expected.
- Do not be afraid to offer "virtual" internships, as there are students who are independent and can deliver great work without having someone constantly watching over them.
- Use the word "strategy" or other relevant buzzwords freely in naming the projects, as these are also the buzz words that students want on their resumes.
- For interns who required too much hand-holding, I usually let them find examples online of what I had asked them to do

so that they could learn what the expected outcome should be. I tried to teach independence. While these interns unfortunately never produced anything of value, I did not mind guiding them through their own learning process.